"George Selgin is one of the leading thinkers on financial and monetary policy in the United States. One need not agree with all, many, or even any of his conclusions to benefit from his deep knowledge of his subjects. His critique of fiscal quantitative easing is no different: a fascinating critical overview of an idea that is gaining traction left, right, and center."

—PETER CONTI-BROWN, author of *The Power and Independence of the Federal Reserve*

"Selgin supports his arguments against fiscal exploitation of the central bank's balance sheet with rich historical evidence and clear economic analysis. As an antidote to fiscal QE, Selgin proposes a corridor framework for monetary policy. This is a must read for anyone making or analyzing monetary policy."

—DARRELL DUFFIE, Dean Witter Distinguished Professor of Finance at Stanford Graduate School of Business

"The dividing line between elected fiscal policymakers and unelected central bankers matters hugely to maintaining a healthy democratic republic. George Selgin's wide-ranging and deep analysis and proposals for how the lines could be redrawn for today's unexpected economic environment deserve wide attention and debate."

—SIR PAUL TUCKER, former Deputy Governor of the Bank of England and author of *Unelected Power: The Quest for Legitimacy in Central Bankii*

"The current 'floor' system of money market management in the USA allows the size of the Fed's balance sheet to be divorced from its mandate to control inflation. This opens the way for some, usually on the political left, to advocate using the Central Bank's balance sheet to fund all kinds of (idealistic) expenditures, 'quasi-fiscal' quantitative easing, thereby avoiding the need for legislative approval and often (mistakenly) perceived as a 'free lunch.' George Selgin advocates a return to a 'corridor' system of money management to avert such dangers."

—CHARLES GOODHART, Emeritus Professor, London School of Economics Financial Markets Group

"While monetary and fiscal policy can be coordinated and conscious of one another, conflating the two would be perilous—for our economy and our democracy. In *The Menace of Fiscal QE*, George Selgin explains why. You should read and heed his warning."

—PETER R. FISHER, Tuck School of Business at Dartmouth, former Under Secretary of the U.S. Treasury

"George Selgin has provided us with an excellent guide to understanding the risks of the Fed's use of Quantitative Easing or QE. It shows how unconventional monetary policies during the crisis have paved the way for fiscal abuse of our central bank's balance sheet. I highly recommend it for anyone with a serious interest in the appropriate interactions of monetary and fiscal policy."

—CHARLES PLOSSER, former President and CEO, Federal Reserve Bank of Philadelphia

THE
MENACE
OF
FISCAL
QE

THE

MENACE

OF

FISCAL

QE

GEORGE SELGIN

CENTER
FOR MONETARY
AND FINANCIAL
ALTERNATIVES

WASHINGTON, DC

ISBN: 978-1-948647-93-9
eISBN: 978-1-948647-94-6

Cover design by Amanda Hudson, Faceout Studio.
Cover imagery from Shutterstock.

Library of Congress Cataloging-in-Publication Data available.

Printed in the United States of America.

Cato Institute
1000 Massachusetts Avenue NW
Washington, DC 20001
www.cato.org

I'm grateful to Darrell Duffie, Andrew Filardo, Peter Fisher, Charles Goodhart, Norbert Michel, Alex Pollock, Charles Plosser, Manmohan Singh, Peter Stella, Nathan Tankus, and Paul Tucker for their valuable suggestions; to Nick Anthony, Nikhil Sridhar, and Tyler Whirty for superb research assistance; and to Thomas Firey, Amanda Griffiths, Jason Kuznicki, and Eleanor O'Connor for editorial assistance.

TABLE OF CONTENTS

1

INTRODUCTION

For some time now, President Donald Trump has been blaming the Federal Reserve for over-tightening monetary policy and calling for it to lower interest rates. But last April he added a new twist to his importuning: a tweet calling not just for lower rates but also for more quantitative easing to help send the U.S. economy "up like a rocket" (Trump 2019).

Although the president's remark was just another instance of his trademark bluster, it happened to coincide with a serious and growing movement to have the Fed and other central banks employ their quantitative easing powers for purposes other than fighting recessions. This movement, favoring what I'll call "fiscal" quantitative easing, or "fiscal QE,"[1] is becoming increasingly popular, and it threatens to

---

[1] Kenneth Rogoff (2019) has recently used the phrase "fiscal QE" to refer to any central bank purchases of private rather than government debt. In contrast, I use it to refer to any large-scale central bank asset purchases undertaken not for strictly macroeconomic purposes but for the sake of either propping up particular firms or markets or funding particular government programs. I further explain my definition below.

erode a valuable division of powers traditionally employed in the modern administrative state. Should the movement continue to grow, and should central banks eventually succumb to it, the consequences are likely to be ones both the general public and central bankers themselves will have reason to regret. Besides fiscal profligacy and a further erosion of central banks' already limited independence, those consequences could also include unwanted inflation and increased central bank and private-sector risk taking.

My specific concern is with the threat that demands for fiscal QE pose to the Federal Reserve and U.S. citizens. I begin by discussing the relationship between conventional and fiscal QE. I then review the history of the fiscal QE movement. Next, I explain how the Fed's postcrisis policy decisions have made it vulnerable to calls for fiscal QE. After that, I consider fiscal QE's potential consequences, showing how, notwithstanding its proponents' claims, it offers no genuine fiscal advantages but is capable of doing great harm. Finally, I consider ways to make the Fed less vulnerable to calls to engage in fiscal QE. I ultimately conclude that Fed officials themselves must take the lead in protecting both the Fed and the public from attempts to abuse its quantitative easing powers. For that reason, I've written this essay with such officials, and others directly involved in shaping Federal Reserve policy, particularly in mind.

Although I argue against quantitative easing as a means for funding government programs, my arguments shouldn't be understood to be ones against the programs themselves. Concerning the merits of any particular government undertaking, I neither venture nor intend to imply any opinion whatsoever.

2

QUANTITATIVE EASING

As used here, quantitative easing (QE) refers to outright central bank asset purchases, and particularly to purchases of long-term assets, beyond those serving to accommodate secular growth in the demand for currency and bank reserves.

Because quantitative easing is generally unnecessary, and because relatively few central banks have made use of it, QE is considered a form of "unconventional" monetary policy. It was unheard of until the Bank of Japan first experimented with large-scale bond purchases in 2001, referring to those purchases by the Japanese equivalent (*ryōteki kin'yū kanwa*) of "quantitative easing." However, because this early Bank of Japan experiment involved purchases of short-term securities only, many do not regard it as an instance of quantitative easing in the now-accepted sense of the term. Only following the 2007–2008 financial crisis did other central banks resort to quantitative easing proper, starting with the Federal Reserve, which began its first of three rounds of quantitative easing at the start of 2009.

So far, central banks have resorted to QE primarily to address deflationary or disinflationary crises, and only after exhausting their capacity to revive spending by conventional means. Until 2012, that generally meant that overnight interest rates were close to their zero lower bounds and therefore could not be driven lower by further central bank asset purchases or otherwise. After 2012, when some central banks began to pay negative interest rates on bank reserves, it meant that policy rates had reached their "effective" lower bounds, below which the responsible authorities weren't prepared to venture.[1]

When banks can earn more interest by simply holding onto excess reserves than by lending those reserves to other banks on the overnight "federal funds" market, central banks can no longer push overnight rates down further, and thereby stimulate additional borrowing and spending, by buying assets so as to place more reserves at banks' disposal. Instead, central banks' asset purchases, and associated additions to the stock of bank reserves, simply lead to corresponding growth in commercial banks' excess reserve holdings. Conventional, expansionary monetary policy therefore ceases to be effective.

The simple premise underlying all arguments for quantitative easing, or what Fed officials prefer to call "large-scale asset purchases," is that even when ordinary central bank asset purchases no longer serve to lower short-term

---

[1] As Miles Kimball (2016) explains, even central bankers unconstrained in their ability to set negative interest rates may be constrained by what they regard as effective lower bounds, owing for example to their fear that excessively negative rates will provoke serious bank disintermediation.

interest rates, extraordinarily large purchases of long-term assets might stimulate spending in other ways.

The various theories concerning just how QE might work are all controversial.[2] And despite Ben Bernanke's 2014 quip that "the problem with QE is it works in practice, but it doesn't work in theory" (Bernanke 2014, 14), claims regarding its past macroeconomic effects are controversial as well.[3] For the purposes of my thesis, however, these controversies are mostly irrelevant: what matters is that the Fed and several other central banks have resorted to QE to combat recessions when they could no longer do so by conventional means, and that many central bankers, including Fed officials, are prepared to resort to it again in the future.

---

[2] On quantitative easing in theory see Bernoth, König, and Raab (2015); Thornton (2015); and Williamson (2017).

[3] Compare, for example, the findings of Gagnon and others (2011a, 2011b) with those of Greenlaw and others (2018); see also Gagnon's (2018) rejoinder to the last.

3

FISCAL QE

Although quantitative easing has thus far been a monetary policy device—that is, a means for assisting central banks in achieving their macroeconomic objectives—it can serve other purposes. In its first and second rounds of QE, for example, the Fed bought large amounts of agency mortgage-backed securities (MBS), not only to stimulate aggregate investment—a standard monetary policy objective—by lowering long-run interest rates, but also to support the housing market.

Although every sort of central bank monetary undertaking has fiscal consequences of some kind, economists typically distinguish between those that have only incidental fiscal consequences and those specifically aimed at supporting particular enterprises, markets, and investments. Only the last undertakings are generally understood to encroach upon "fiscal" policy. Thus Charles Plosser (2012) observes, "When the Fed engages in targeted credit programs that seek to alter the allocation of credit across markets . . . it is engaging in fiscal policy and has breached the traditional boundaries established between the fiscal authorities and the central bank."

It's generally agreed that central bank purchases of private financial or real assets, apart from ones required for daily operations, breach the boundaries to which Plosser refers. But by some accounts QE can breach those boundaries even when it involves purchases of government securities only. The Fed might, for example, resort to quantitative easing not for the sake of meeting its monetary policy objectives when short-term rates are at their effective lower bounds, but simply as a method for financing government spending. This possibility was acknowledged by Bernanke in February 2011, when he testified before the House Budget Committee. Asked by then-Committee Chair Paul Ryan whether the Fed's second round of large-scale asset purchases, colloquially called QE2, was not simply an example of debt monetization, Bernanke (2011, 15) replied:

> No, sir. Monetization would involve a permanent increase in the money supply to basically pay the government's bills through money creation. What we are doing here is a temporary measure which will be reversed so that at the end of this process, the money supply will be normalized, the amount of the Fed's balance sheet will be normalized, and there will be no permanent increase, either in money outstanding, or in the Fed's balance sheet.[1]

---

[1] David Andolfatto and Li Li (2013, 1–2) likewise claim that the difference between debt monetization and nonfiscal QE hinges on whether the Fed's government security purchases are permanent or temporary. In the latter case, they say, "the Fed is not monetizing government debt—it is simply managing the supply of the monetary base in accordance with the goals set by its dual mandate." This distinction begs the question: if the Fed acquires Treasury debt and chooses to hold it for an indefinite period, at what point, if ever, may its purchases be regarded as constituting debt monetization?

As Bernanke (2016) explains elsewhere, Milton Friedman's (1969) "helicopter money" idea is itself really just a particular type of debt monetization with money creation serving to finance particular government spending programs or tax cuts or both. In practice, it makes no difference whether the funding takes the form of direct Fed credits to the Treasury General Account or Fed purchases of an equivalent amount of new Treasury debt.

To classify large-scale debt monetization that doesn't involve support of particular spending programs as fiscal QE isn't to say that such monetization is necessarily undesirable. While large-scale monetization outside of the zero lower bound tends to be inflationary,[2] when undertaken at the zero lower bound, or in a "floor" system in which interest on reserves serves to implement the Fed's policy rate target, it amounts to a noninflationary substitution of short-term bank reserves for longer-term Treasury debt. In theory such a substitution might be beneficial. (Later I'll consider whether actual circumstances are likely to warrant it.)

Quantitative easing that's primarily aimed at combating a recession or countering low inflation when rates reach their lower bounds, but that's intended to serve fiscal ends as well, is "quasi-fiscal." Quasi-fiscal QE has been relatively common. The Fed's MBS purchases have already been mentioned. The European Central Bank's large-scale asset purchases included purchases of both corporate and "covered" bonds, meaning collateralized bonds

---

[2] Whether monetization is or isn't inflationary ultimately depends on whether it drives interest rates below their noninflationary or "natural" levels.

issued by banks and mortgage lenders, as well as purchases of troubled sovereign debt. The Bank of Japan's various quantitative easings have made it Japan's largest owner of exchange-traded funds (ETFs). The Bank of Switzerland has also been an aggressive purchaser of equity shares. These are but the most recent examples. Earlier instances might also be mentioned, such as the Hong Kong Monetary Authority's decision, during the 1987 stock market crash, to employ its Exchange Fund to support the Hong Kong futures market.[3]

Proposals for helicopter money have, thus far, also been proposals for quasi-fiscal QE, to be employed solely during economic downturns, and then only when conventional monetary policy options either are unavailable or prove ineffective. Typical in this respect is the recent BlackRock Investment Institute proposal calling for the establishment of a "standing emergency fiscal authority" to be activated only "when monetary policy is tapped out and inflation is expected to systematically undershoot its target" (Bartsch and others 2019, 2).

Both the theory and the practice of quasi-fiscal quantitative easing have nonetheless helped to spur on the movement for *strictly* fiscal QE, meaning quantitative easing whose purpose is to prop up particular markets or finance government undertakings *rather than* to combat recession whenever conventional monetary policy can't do so. Although quasi-fiscal QE may serve as a "slippery slope" toward its strictly fiscal counterpart, and some of the risks posed by strictly fiscal QE are posed by quasi-fiscal QE

---

[3] I'm grateful to Darrell Duffie for reminding me of this episode.

as well, this study is mainly concerned with the possibility that the Fed may eventually be compelled to engage in *strictly* fiscal QE.

Unlike quasi-fiscal QE, strictly fiscal QE is as yet only a hypothetical possibility.[4] But growing support for it, together with its potentially serious consequences, warrants an assessment to determine whether it can ever be beneficial and, if not, to explore ways to prevent it.

---

[4] Although, in October 2019, the Federal Reserve announced a new round of security purchases, with planned purchases of $60 billion each month lasting until the second quarter of 2020, Fed officials insist that, because these purchases are aimed at addressing an apparent reserve shortage rather than at achieving any further monetary stimulus, they should not be considered an instance of quantitative easing (Smialek 2019b). The purchases may nonetheless be seen by some as serving as a precedent for strictly fiscal QE programs.

4

THE FISCAL QE MOVEMENT

In calling for more quantitative easing long after the United States had emerged from the Great Recession, and at a time when short-run interest rates were well above zero, President Trump joined a growing movement that's almost as old as the Fed's first round of quantitative easing.

Yet the first fiscal QE proposal of any significance was British, not American. Like many subsequent fiscal QE proposals, it was a brainchild of the political left, and particularly of green politics. In 2010, British economist Richard Murphy and Green New Deal Group convener Colin Hines (2010) proposed that the Bank of England, which had begun its own QE program in March 2009, undertake a further round of easing that Murphy called "Green QE2." Unlike the Bank of England's ongoing QE program, which was aimed at making British banks more liquid, green QE was supposed to finance an early British version of the Green New Deal, with its proposed "massive investment in renewable energy and wider environmental transformation" (Green New Deal Group 2008).

In retrospect, says Tony Yates (2015b) (who took part in the Bank of England's original quantitative easing efforts), proposals like Murphy and Hines's were an almost inevitable consequence of the Bank of England's nonfiscal QE effort:

> As the public grappled with the "print money, buy assets" meme, it's only natural to wonder why if the Bank can buy those sterile old bonds, it can't buy something more useful for us all. Such worries were alive and well when I was in the Bank of England. And they were not helped by the UK Treasury using the "profits" from these purchases (which one would expect to be reversed later, as assets are sold by the BoE) to reduce its routine borrowing.

For some years nothing came of Murphy and Hines's proposal. In the meantime the New Economics Foundation, a British think tank devoted to creating "a new economy that by 2040 works for people and within environmental limits" (New Economics Foundation 2016), published a proposal for "strategic" quantitative easing. The proposal offered several possible plans for "targeted" QE (Ryan-Collins and others 2013). Among these were plans to have the Bank of England acquire UK banks' nonperforming assets; to have it directly fund "large-scale infrastructure investment in transport, energy, and housing"; and to have it pay for the British government's Green Deal.[1] Somewhat later several British academics,

---

[1] The last of these was a British government policy initiative, not to be confused with the British Green New Deal, aimed at funding the retrofitting of private buildings to make them more energy efficient.

including Adair Turner (Reichlin, Turner, and Woodford 2019), Simon Wren-Lewis (2015a), and John Muellbauer (2014), began urging central banks to put the helicopter money idea into practice, with Muellbauer referring to his plan—calling for the European Central Bank to send a €500 check to every adult European citizen—as "QE for the People."

Because they were all aimed at promoting recovery from the Great Recession, and their emphasis was on altering the use rather than the total extent of central bank funding, these proposed programs were quasi-fiscal rather than strictly fiscal in nature. They served nonetheless to whet the British left's appetite for strictly fiscal QE.

That idea gained the limelight when, during the 2015 Labour Leadership contest, Jeremy Corbyn resurrected the Murphy-Hines proposal, while taking a leaf from Muellbauer's as well by calling his version "People's" quantitative easing. Under Corbyn's plan the Bank of England would buy bonds issued by a state-owned "National Investment Bank" (NIB) charged with "providing funding on a sufficient scale to meet the needs and potential of the UK's small and medium-sized enterprises," among other things. "Over the ten year policy horizon," the NIB prospectus says, it "would conduct ten annual bond issues, which would expand the NIB balance sheet to approximately £250 billion by the tenth year" (Calvert Jump and others 2017, 8, 10). That a "ten year policy horizon" far exceeds the length of even the longest-known economic downturn underscores this proposal's overarching fiscal (as opposed to macroeconomic) purpose.

People's QE won support from some prominent media commentators, including Robert Skidelsky (2015) and Matthew Klein (2015). But it was sharply criticized by several equally prominent members of the Labour Party (Watt 2015; Elliot 2015) who feared it would ultimately lead to higher inflation and interest rates. The plan was also roundly condemned by Bank of England officials, including Governor Mark Carney, who worried that it would undermine the Bank's independence. According to Tony Yates (2015a), that independence "prevents the government being [sic] tempted to finance pet projects with money-printing, thus avoiding the politically tricky decision to borrow," thereby helping to "smooth the booms and busts of the business cycle."

Though he favored helicopter money as a means for combatting the Great Recession, Simon Wren-Lewis (2015b) also opposed the plan:

> The idea behind helicopter money is to provide a tool for the central bank to use when interest rate changes are no longer possible or effective. With an independent central bank, that means that they [central bank authorities], not the government, get to decide when helicopter money happens. In contrast, if your goal is to increase either public or private investment (or both) for a prolonged period, then its timing and amount should be something the government decides. . . . For that reason, Corbyn's QE looks like one of those ideas that is superficially attractive because it seems to kill two birds with one stone, but on reflection turns out to be a bad idea. If we want to keep an independent central bank we do not

want the government putting the bank under pressure to do QE because the government wants more investment.

Among U.S. officials, Ben Bernanke raised a similar objection to People's QE (2016, 4):

> From a purely economic perspective, People's QE would . . . be equivalent to a money-financed tax cut (Friedman's original helicopter drop, although perhaps more targeted). The problem with this policy . . . is not its economic logic but its political legitimacy: The distribution of what are effectively tax rebates should be subject to legislative approval, not determined unilaterally by the central bank.

In fact, for reasons I'll come to, the "economic logic" of People's QE is itself suspect, particularly when it is offered as a strictly fiscal plan, rather than one to be employed solely when the Bank of England's policy rate is at its effective lower bound.

People's QE has nevertheless gained many adherents, some of whom consider it overly timid. A 2018 *Guardian* editorial (*The Guardian* 2018), for example, suggested that Corbyn's plan could be improved upon by instructing "the central bank . . . to hand over funds to a state body so it could buy services and goods without issuing debt." A few years earlier, Frances Coppola (2015) also found that Corbyn's plan too limited. "I fail to see," she wrote, "why investing in the economy should be dependent on there being a recession. I also fail to see why it has to wait for a future government. Her Majesty's opposition should make the case for significant borrowing for investment now."

In her recently published book on People's QE, Coppola (2019, 67–68) takes up the same theme, distinguishing between People's QE aimed at short-term stimulus and QE aimed at longer-term government financing or "economic rebalancing"—categories corresponding to what I've termed quasi-fiscal and strictly fiscal QE. While favoring either sort of QE, she shows particular enthusiasm for the second. Long-term People's QE, she says, could "help the world address" (presumably by financing) "three major challenges that threaten human life as we know it," namely, the challenges of aging, automation, and climate change. She wonders, indeed, whether, "instead of merely being an ad-hoc stimulus," People's QE might eventually become "the principal means of managing the economy" (Coppola 2019, 121).

A QE Student Debt Jubilee

By U.S. quantitative easing standards, Jeremy Corbyn's £250 billion QE proposal was paltry. But Corbyn's plan would ultimately inspire a U.S. counterpart that was anything but paltry. It did so, however, only after a lag of several years. In the meantime, the U.S. Green Party came up with its own, quite different fiscal QE proposal.

Despite having been around since 2001, and despite having developed its own Green New Deal in 2006, the U.S. Green Party itself never proposed having the Fed directly fund a Green New Deal. Instead, several Green

Party members suggested that the Fed use QE to solve the student debt problem. That idea may have originated with *Web of Debt* author Ellen Brown (2011), who suggested that the Fed "foot the bill" for a student loan "jubilee":

> Commentators say that debt forgiveness is impossible. . . . But there is one deep pocket that could pull it off—the Federal Reserve. In its first quantitative easing program (QE1), the Fed removed $1.3 trillion in toxic assets from the books of Wall Street banks. For QE4, it could remove $1 trillion in toxic debt from the backs of millions of students.

At least one think tank, the Roosevelt Institute, lent its support to Brown's proposal (Mabie 2012), observing that "the more financial assets the Federal Reserve purchases, the more complete the process of debt forgiveness will be."[2]

In May 2013, Sen. Elizabeth Warren (D-MA) introduced the Bank on Students Loan Fairness Act (S. 897). That act called for the Fed to finance student loans, using the Department of Education as an intermediary, at the same low interest rate it was then charging banks for discount-window loans (U.S. Congress, Senate 2013). In defense of the plan Warren and then-Rep. John Tierney (D-MA),

---

[2] A study by several Modern Monetary Theorists (Fullwiler et al. 2018) concludes, in contrast, that having the Fed acquire student debt would have "the same consequences for the federal government's budget position as a government-led program—that is, there is no 'free lunch' that avoids the budgetary implications of cancelling student debt."

the measure's cosponsor, compared it to the Fed's first round of quantitative easing. The Fed, Tierney said,

> can expand its balance sheet by buying all the assets it likes. The Fed bought over $1 trillion in "toxic" mortgage-backed securities in QE 1, and reportedly turned a profit on them. It could just as easily buy $1 trillion in student debt and refinance it at 0.75%. (Brown 2013)[3]

A similar plan became notorious when, in 2015, Green Party presidential candidate Jill Stein, perhaps drawing on Brown's suggestion, proposed using the Federal Reserve's quantitative easing powers to cancel what was by then "$1.3 trillion in predatory student debt" (Jill Stein for President 2015a). The details of Stein's proposal—among other things she seemed to believe that the president has the authority to compel the Fed to take part in it—drew a withering rebuke from "Last Week Tonight" host John Oliver. Her campaign's response— that despite Oliver's criticisms, "it is technically possible,

---

[3] Responding to Senator Warren's proposal, Beth Akers and Matthew Chingos (2013) of the Brookings Institution wrote:

> Sen. Warren's proposal should be quickly dismissed as a cheap political gimmick. It proposes only a one-year change to the rate on one kind of federal student loan, confuses market interest rates on long-term loans (such as the 10-year Treasury rate) with the Federal Reserve's Discount Window (used to make short-term loans to banks), and does not reflect the administrative costs and default risk that increase the costs of the federal student loan program.

The more recent Bank on Students Emergency Loan Refinancing Act (H.R. 1707), sponsored by Senator Warren and Rep. Joe Courtney (D-CT), doesn't involve Federal Reserve funding.

even if politically difficult, for the Fed to play a role in student debt forgiveness" (Jill Stein for President 2015b)—was, however, correct.

The U.S. Green New Deal

After the 2016 U.S. presidential election, some Democrats began developing their own Green New Deal. In February 2019, Rep. Alexandria Ocasio-Cortez (D-NY) and Sen. Ed Markey (D-MA) unveiled their Green New Deal (GND) resolution (U.S. Congress, Senate 2019). The resolution called for a decade-long spending program aimed not just at "repairing and upgrading the infrastructure in the United States," but also at supplying "all people of the United States" with a guaranteed job, high-quality health care, adequate housing, energy-efficient buildings, improved and environmentally friendly public transportation, and emission-free energy, among other things.

According to a thumbnail estimate by economist Noah Smith (2019), the GND could easily end up costing upward of $6 trillion, or perhaps 34 percent of U.S. gross domestic product (GDP), for *each* of its 10 years.[4] That potential expense raises two obvious questions: where are all the needed *real resources* to come from, and where is all the *money* to come from? Some Green New Deal proponents answer the first question by claiming that the GND will rely heavily on presently unemployed resources, and that it will eventually boost productivity enough to create more resources than

---

[4] It should be noted that Smith's estimate includes the cost of a universal basic income plan that, though part of Ocasio-Cortez's original Green New Deal draft, was removed from the final version.

it consumes. They answer the second question by suggesting that the Fed will be bound to supply the necessary amounts. "We will pay for the Green New Deal the same way we paid for the original New Deal, World War II, the 2008 bank bailout, *extended quantitative easing* programs, all our current wars," Ocasio-Cortez said in a February 2019 blog post that was subsequently taken down. "The Federal Reserve can extend credit to power these projects" (Ip 2019).

The MMT Connection

I wrote "will be bound to supply" because Representative Ocasio-Cortez and some other supporters of the U.S. Green New Deal have been influenced by proponents of Modern Monetary Theory (MMT), who insist that the Fed is not just materially *capable* of supplying any amount of money the government wants, but that it can't help but do so. As Stephanie Kelton, Andrés Bernal, and Greg Carlock (2018) put it, "our government already pays for everything by creating new money":

> As a monopoly supplier of U.S. currency with full financial sovereignty, the federal government is not like a household or even a business. When Congress authorizes spending, it sets off a sequence of actions. Federal agencies, such as the Department of Defense or Department of Energy, enter into contracts and begin spending. As the checks go out, the government's bank—the Federal Reserve—clears the payments by crediting the seller's bank account with digital dollars.[5]

---

[5] On the broadening appeal of Modern Monetary Theory, see Cohen (2019).

It follows, Kelton, Bernal, and Carlock argue, that "the federal government can spend money on public priorities without raising revenue, and it won't wreck the nation's economy to do so. That may sound radical, but it's not. It's how the U.S. economy has been functioning for nearly half a century. That's the power of the public purse."

Kelton, Bernal, and Carlock are not so much *recommending* that the Fed fund government spending as claiming that it *inevitably* does so. For that reason, they can't really be said to favor resorting to QE over other methods for financing such spending. Their perspective is rather that the Fed never has to take steps deliberately aimed at funding government programs.[6] Statements like theirs are nevertheless all-too-readily understood to imply that fiscal QE, or something like it, is both a politically legitimate and an expedient, if not "painless," way to finance major government programs.

Is the Fed really bound to create money to accommodate any conceivable level of government spending? Has it no say in the matter? It's true that the Fed executes payments on behalf of the federal government. It's also true

---

[6] In their in-depth study on funding the GND, Modern Monetary Theorists Yeva Nersisyan and L. Randall Wray (2019, 7) make this point explicitly:

> We already have the financial wherewithal needed to afford whatever is technologically possible. We do not need to go hat-in-hand to rich folks to get them to pay for it. We do not have to beggar our grandkids to pay for it. We do not have to borrow from China to pay for it. *We do not have to get the Fed to "print money" to pay for it.* . . . Follow the normal procedures that the Fed and Treasury have developed. That is how you pay for it. (emphasis added)

that whatever money the government spends must have been created by the Fed. But despite what Kelton et al. suggest, it doesn't follow that the Fed passively accommodates government spending. Instead, the government can keep spending only so long as the necessary funds are present in the Treasury's account at the Fed—that is, the Treasury General Account or TGA. The Treasury isn't allowed to overdraw that account. Nor does any arrangement compel the Fed to automatically replenish it once it runs out (Selgin 2019b). Instead, the government has to replenish it using proceeds from taxation or borrowing.

As for the Fed's role in assisting government borrowing, the MMT view seems to downplay, or to treat as irrelevant, the difference between the Federal Reserve's conduct before the 1951 Treasury-Fed Accord and its conduct since then, and particularly during both the Volcker disinflation and the subsequent Great Moderation. Before the accord, and during World War II especially, the Fed was committed to "pegging" the rate of interest at a fixed, low rate, at which it passively accommodated the federal government's spending needs. It has since been free to adjust its interest rate target with other objectives, and inflation control in particular, in mind.[7] Were the Fed to accommodate GND spending as it accommodated spending during World War II, it would risk high inflation, or (alternatively) a revival of WWII-style price controls. In short, unless Congress adjusts its overall level of deficit spending with macroeconomic stability in mind, the Fed can *either* tend to

---

[7] I discuss the 1951 Treasury-Fed Accord and some of its consequences below.

that stability *or* passively fund very large increases in government spending. It can't do both.[8]

Thus, although it may be true that the Treasury can generally borrow funds to cover its expenses at *some* price, it isn't the case, as Kelton and some other Modern Monetary Theorists suggest, that government spending inevitably results in corresponding money creation, by quantitative easing or otherwise. At present the Fed remains free to limit its security purchases as needed to maintain interest targets of its choosing and to constrain government spending by means of its target choices. Because the Treasury is legally barred from overdrawing its Federal Reserve Account, the Fed is free so far to limit the growth of its balance sheet as needed to contain inflation, or for other reasons, forcing Congress to cover its expenses either by

---

[8] While Modern Monetary Theory is sometimes interpreted as favoring reliance upon fiscal policy, including increased taxation, to check inflation, some of its proponents doubt that this would be necessary. "From our view," Scott Fullwiler, Rohan Grey, and Nathan Tankus (2019) write, "excess demand is rarely the cause of inflation. Whether it's businesses raising profit margins or passing on costs, or it's Wall Street speculating on commodities or houses, there are a range of sources of inflation that aren't caused by the general state of demand and aren't best regulated by aggregate demand policies." Instead, they add, "alternative tools" are needed "to manage the power of big business and ensure their pricing policies are consistent with public purpose." Although Fullwiler, Grey, and Tankus don't specifically refer to wage and price controls, their arguments here resemble ones long put forth in favor of such controls, and they are subject to the same criticisms. In particular, they seem vulnerable to Milton Friedman's (1966, 57) observation that "Insofar as market power has anything to do with possible inflation, what is important is not the *level* of market power, but whether market power is *growing* or not. If there is an existing state of monopolies all over the lot, but the degree of monopoly has not been increasing, this monopoly power will not and cannot be a source of pressure for inflation."

collecting taxes or by competing with other borrowers for available credit.

While certain MMT writings understate the degree to which the government is constrained by present Federal Reserve practices, those writings do accurately describe the sort of arrangements that many Modern Monetary Theorists consider ideal. The question that concerns us here isn't whether the Fed is presently bound to fund the federal government's expenses, as some Modern Monetary Theorists suggest. The question is whether the Fed, perhaps owing in part to MMT's influence, might be compelled to do so in the future, through explicit legislation or otherwise, and particularly whether its quantitative easing capacity might, or should, be exploited for this purpose.

5

THE FAST ACT:
A WORRISOME PRECEDENT

The possibility that Congress might compel the Fed to use its quantitative easing powers to finance a Green New Deal, or some other ambitious spending project, may today seem too hypothetical to be a cause of concern. But while it has never attempted to force the Fed to resort to QE, or to pay for environmental programs, Congress *has* forced the Fed to pay for transportation infrastructure improvements, thereby establishing a precedent that could join other developments in helping to pave the way toward compulsory fiscal QE.

The Peterson Plan

The first person to propose that the Fed foot part of the bill for infrastructure improvements appears to have been bond analyst Cate Long. Writing for Reuters, Long (2012) suggested that, instead of trying to prop up the mortgage market or hold down long-term interest rates, "the Fed should turn to buying infrastructure bonds to rebuild America's energy grid, bridges, roads, rail systems and ports." Somewhat later Eric Peterson (2013), then the deputy administrator of the Transportation Department's Research and Innovative Technology Administration, proposed having the Fed devote some of its then-ongoing QE to financing improvements in this country's transportation infrastructure—a quasi-fiscal version of Long's proposal.

According to Peterson, the advantage of QE is that it overcomes the hurdle of the executive and legislative branches' insistence "on treating infrastructure in the budgetary and appropriations process of the Federal Government the same way they treat the purchase of office supplies and equipment or government workers' salaries":

> If the U.S. had an infrastructure bank, or better yet, if the Federal Reserve were to direct its quantitative easing resources toward infrastructure projects, the massive inventory of needed and planned transportation infrastructure projects could be addressed quickly, securing both a brighter future for America's workforce, a better future for America's competitive position in the world, and brighter prospects for improving the mobility of the nation while redressing the environmental impacts that the nation's current transportation produces. (Peterson 2013)

Peterson's plan would have had the Fed "redirect" $28 billion a month of its ongoing QE initiative to infrastructure spending, presumably by having it purchase that value of U.S. Department of Transportation private activity bonds (U.S. Department of Transportation, n.d.).

Raiding the Fed's Surplus Account

Although it never acted on Peterson's proposal, Congress eventually came up with a different way to make the Fed pay for transportation infrastructure improvements: raiding its surplus account. As Helen Fessenden (2015, 4) explains, when, in preparing what became the 2015 Fixing America's Surface Transportation (FAST) Act,

> lawmakers couldn't agree on how to boost financing via traditional means—including raising the gas tax—they found their source within the Fed instead. Although senior Fed officials objected that using a central bank to fund specific fiscal needs would set a worrisome precedent, the strong political momentum to complete the long-stalled bill persuaded large majorities in both parties to throw their support behind the underlying legislation.

Buried within the FAST Act was a provision capping the Federal Reserve Banks' aggregate surplus, which is supposed to help cushion the Fed against potential losses, at $10 billion. Anything above that amount was to be "transferred to the Board of Governors of the Federal Reserve System for transfer to the Secretary of the Treasury for deposit in the general fund of the Treasury" to help pay for transportation infrastructure improvements (U.S. Congress, House 2015).

When the FAST Act took effect in 2016, Fed surpluses added up to almost $30 billion. So the Fed was obliged to immediately transfer almost $20 billion to the Treasury. As Robert Heller (2016) observed in *American*

Banker, the transfer left the Fed with a remarkably thin capital cushion:

> Given the size of the Federal Reserve System's balance sheet of $4.5 trillion, a cap on the surplus account of only $10 billion amounts to a paltry 0.2% of the Fed's total balance sheet. Even if one adds the $30 billion of paid-in capital owned by the member banks, the total capital stock of the entire Federal Reserve System is now less than $40 billion—still less than 1% of the Fed's balance sheet. No private bank would be allowed to continue in business with such meager capital reserves.

Nor was that one-time transfer all that Congress extracted from the Fed. As long as the Fed's surplus didn't fall below $10 billion it had to hand over all earnings in excess of those limits—a total of almost $17 billion over five years, including $2.8 billion in diverted dividends. Congress therefore didn't just raid the Fed's surplus: it severely limited its ability to reduce its remittances to the Treasury for the sake of either paying dividends or augmenting its capital.

Running Dry

While the FAST Act was still in the works, then–Fed Vice Chair Stanley Fischer pointed out the dangers of having Congress use the Fed "to provide revenue to fund specific government initiatives, which amounts to quasi-fiscal policy." Doing so, he said, "has manifold implications not only for central-bank independence but also for the quality of fiscal-policy decisions" (Lawler 2015). Janet Yellen also complained that "Financing federal fiscal spending by tapping the resources of the Federal Reserve sets a bad precedent" (Fessenden 2015, 6). Helen Fessenden agrees:

> Generally speaking, if central banks are forced to subordinate monetary policy to fiscal or political needs, politicians could compel them to print money, which in turn could spur inflation. In this particular case, warnings from Fed officials focused on the concern that Congress could turn to the Fed in future budget battles rather than making fiscal trade-offs (cutting spending or raising taxes) on its own. (Fessenden 2015, 5)

The FAST Act's raid on the Fed's capital surplus actually had precedents of its own. In 1933, Congress used half of the Fed's surplus to capitalize the Federal Deposit Insurance Corporation (FDIC); and in 1993, it passed the Deficit Reduction Act, which among other measures withdrew $213 million from the Fed's surplus account to meet its budget reconciliation targets (Goodfriend 1994, 576–77). Still, Yellen had a point, as became obvious when, in a 2018 budget deal, Congress raided the Fed's surplus again (Condon 2018), grabbing another $2.5 billion and leaving the Fed with $7.5 billion, or just *0.16 percent* of its assets at the time.

Congress's willingness to raid the Fed's surplus for revenue is significant, not just because it shows that the Fed isn't immune to such congressional interference, but because it illustrates Congress's willingness to force the Fed to fund its priorities *even when doing so isn't really fiscally advantageous*. For example, although the Fed's 1993 surplus transfer appeared to supply the Treasury with supplementary funds, it actually did no such thing. As the late Marvin Goodfriend (1994) explains, because the Fed financed the transfer by selling an equivalent value of Treasury securities, it had to reduce its remittances to the Treasury accordingly. The outcome was therefore the same as if the Treasury had issued that much new debt directly to the public. So, while the transfer allowed the federal government to record increased revenues and smaller deficits for two years, that was only because the Fed's security sales—its "negative debt monetization," as it were—didn't show up in the Treasury's account as extra borrowing. Congress's larger-scale 2015 raid on the Fed's surplus was equally fruitless, amounting, Ben Bernanke (2015) complained, to mere "budgetary sleight of hand."

Whether raiding the Fed's capital is truly advantageous or not, Congress can secure only so much funding that way. But, as already noted, the FAST Act doesn't merely serve as a precedent for raiding the Fed's capital. It also supplies a precedent for tapping into the Fed's other resources, including its quantitative easing powers, which, unlike the Fed's capital, seem unlimited. As we'll see, the government's actual gains from fiscal QE are likely to be as illusory as those secured by its capital raids. But because appearances can matter more to Congress than reality, that won't necessarily prevent it from hungrily eyeing a seemingly inexhaustible treasure trove.

6

FOUNDATIONS OF THE
FED'S INDEPENDENCE

The FAST Act precedent, growing support for a Green New Deal, the influence of MMT, the quasi-fiscal nature of the Fed's past QE programs, Congress's awareness of the Fed's vast powers of quantitative easing, and the Fed's decision to permanently retain those vast powers: together these form a volatile mix that threatens to propel strictly fiscal QE from theory to practice, eroding the Fed's fragile independence in the process. And given its present operating procedures and framework, the Fed cannot be counted on to successfully resist this threat.

It's true that the present Fed administration seems to have little appetite for fiscal QE: In response to suggestions that the Fed might fund the Green New Deal, Fed Chair Jerome Powell said, "Our role is not to provide support for particular policies. . . . It is to try to achieve maximum employment and stable prices" (Cox 2019a). But a future Fed might prove less determined to resist the idea—assuming it doesn't embrace it.

To appreciate the danger to Fed independence that mounting calls for fiscal QE pose, it's necessary to place that independence in its historical context.

The Roots of Central Bank Independence

There is, of course, nothing new about governments wanting central banks to pay their bills. More than a few central banks, including some of the earliest, were established for the express purpose of replenishing royal, parliamentary, or consular coffers.[1] But while governments have often treated their central banks as sources of fiscal favors, over time, as other revenue sources have improved, they've tended to do so less frequently, particularly in times of peace.

For several centuries, central banks' commitment to redeem their liabilities in silver or gold constrained their accommodation of government spending. Over time that constraint was reinforced by the understanding that central

---

[1] Concerning the Bank of England H. S. Foxwell writes:

> This Bank was, above all others, perhaps, in its origin and development, emphatically the servant of the State. Arising out of a State loan, it was cradled in a Ways and Means Act dealing with the tonnage duties imposed to provide interest on the loan; and in early days was nicknamed the "Tunnage Bank." (1911, 5)

According to André Liesse (1909, 17), Napoleon Bonaparte saw to the Bank of France's establishment because he "felt that the Treasury needed money, and wanted to have under his hand an establishment which he could compel to meet his wishes." See also Selgin (2016). Concerning governments' tendency to exploit early public banks, whatever their intended purpose, for fiscal gains, see Roberds and Velde (2014).

banks had broad duties apart from catering to their sponsoring governments' fiscal needs. As gold standards gave way to fiat monies, temporarily during World War I and permanently afterward, that understanding itself became a crucial constraint against the abuse of central banks for fiscal purposes. Some central banks also gained considerable formal independence from their governments, in part by having governing bodies in which neither elected officials nor appointees to other government bureaus took part.

The Treasury-Fed Accord

The Fed's current and still limited independence was hard won. During its first decades, it was often a mere handmaiden to the U.S. Treasury. During World War II in particular, the Fed agreed to "peg" interest rates on Treasury bills and bonds so that the government could finance the war relatively cheaply. That meant giving up control of the size and content of its asset portfolio (Romero 2013) and agreeing to buy Treasury securities even when doing so might cause unwanted inflation. In short, the Fed really did function much as some Modern Monetary Theorists suggest it functions, or ought to function, today, passively creating new money to accommodate the federal government's spending, while allowing the government to dictate its interest rate settings.

During the Korean War the Fed's cordial understanding with the government unraveled. In October 1950, fearing inflation and in defiance of the Treasury, the Federal Open Market Committee (FOMC) raised the interest rate on Treasury bills, though it still honored its commitment to peg the rate on longer-term Treasury bonds. Then, as the war intensified and the inflation rate rose sharply, Fed officials realized that by continuing to honor the latter commitment the Fed was serving as "an engine of inflation" (Hetzel and Leach 2001, 43). At last, on February 19, 1951, Fed officials let the Treasury know that they were "no longer willing to maintain the existing situation in the Government security market" (Hetzel and Leach 2001, 49). The announcement launched negotiations between the Fed and the Treasury that would eventually lead to the compromise now known as the Treasury-Fed Accord.

The details of that accord needn't concern us.[2] What matters is that it ushered in the current arrangement: instead of pegging interest rates at the Treasury's behest, the Fed was left free to adjust its rate target routinely to whatever levels it considers consistent with its monetary policy aims.

The Great Inflation: A Watershed

Although the Treasury-Fed Accord freed the Fed from any formal obligation to peg interest rates, it fell far short of securing the Fed's complete independence or otherwise making it immune to pressure to help the government fund its budget.[3] During the 1960s, such pressure intensified as spending on the Vietnam War and President Lyndon Johnson's Great Society programs put increasing

---

[2] For these see Mueller (1952, 596–99).

[3] On the Fed's limited and precarious independence see Conti-Brown (2016) and Binder and Spindel (2017).

strains on the U.S. Treasury. That pressure combined with several other factors—the influence of a new Keynesian orthodoxy wedded to the belief that higher inflation meant reduced unemployment; President Richard Nixon's determination to have the Fed enhance his reelection prospects; an especially pliable Fed chairman (Arthur Burns); and, later, OPEC's oil embargo—gave rise to the Great Inflation.[4]

The Great Inflation has been called "the greatest failure of American macroeconomic policy in the postwar period" (Bryan 2013). Yet the ultimate consequence of that failure was a change in both expert and lay opinion that ultimately helped strengthen the Fed's independence. As the U.S. inflation rate rose to double-digit territory, while unemployment, instead of continuing to decline, rose well above its level in the early 1960s, fighting inflation came to be seen as the Fed's overarching responsibility, even if the fight meant a temporary, further, spike in unemployment.

The story of Paul Volcker's successful leadership of that fight is presumably well known. In any event, it's relevant here only because of the way it helped strengthen the Fed's independence while also driving home the lessons that inflation is indeed a monetary phenomenon, and that central banks cannot simply accommodate their sponsoring governments' fiscal demands without sacrificing control of it.

---

[4] On President Nixon's influence on Burns's Fed, see Abrams (2006). On the part that pressure from both Congress and the executive branch played, see Weise (2012). For a very good telling of the whole story of the Great Inflation, see Samuelson (2008).

The Fed's reinforced independence didn't mean that revenue-hungry governments would no longer have reason to try to abuse its money-creating powers. As Christopher Sims (2016, 6) explains:

> Short-sighted politicians might find it attractive to vote for debt-financed expenditures and, to avoid this generating high interest rates, to require the central bank to purchase the debt. The high inflation such policies generate comes (at least at first) with a delay, perhaps after the next election.

Still, the post–Great Inflation conventional wisdom that excessive Fed debt monetization fuels inflation supplied the Fed and other central banks with a powerful argument for refusing to take part in it. The result has been a much-enhanced Fed commitment to inflation control that few political authorities dare to openly challenge.

7

INDEPENDENCE AND THE FED'S PRECRISIS FRAMEWORK

The connection between excessive Fed debt monetization and inflation isn't inevitable. Instead, it depends on the Fed's operating system or framework—the particular devices it uses to regulate the growth of money and credit. Although various options are available, the debate these days is mainly between proponents of a "corridor" system on one hand and those favoring a "floor" system on the other.

In a corridor system, bank reserves bear only a modest return, if not a return of zero, so banks tend to keep as few reserves as possible. The central bank in turn must limit the availability of reserves to achieve its intermediate interest rate target and, ultimately, to regulate inflation. The scarcity of reserves gives rise to an active private overnight market for reserves—the federal funds market—in which banks with excess reserves lend to those in danger of falling short of them. The central bank sets an overnight rate target somewhere (typically halfway) between the modest rate paid on reserves and its emergency lending rate. It then uses daily open-market operations to fine-tune the stock of reserves, so as to limit movement in the actual overnight rate within the corridor's lower and upper (interest on reserves and overnight lending rate) boundaries.

In a floor system, in contrast, reserves typically earn a return equal to or exceeding the central bank's overnight rate target. Banks are therefore willing to accumulate excess reserves. The central bank in turn creates an abundance of such reserves sufficient, in theory, to render interbank borrowing unnecessary. In most floor systems the interest rate paid on reserves serves as both the central bank's rate target and its instrument of monetary control. To tighten money, the central bank raises the rate, causing other market money rates to rise. To loosen money, it does the opposite. Routine open-market operations are neither necessary nor effective. Consequently, *the often assumed relationship between balance-sheet expansion and inflation is not present in a floor system.*

The Fed relied on a corridor framework of sorts throughout the Great Moderation—the period of relative macroeconomic stability that lasted from the mid-1980s until the 2007–2008 financial crisis. Because the Fed did not yet pay interest on bank reserves, while its rate target settings and discount rate varied, the Fed's corridor was unorthodox in that its fixed zero interest rate on reserves made it both asymmetrical and of time-varying width. The pre-2008 Fed system nevertheless resembled more orthodox corridor systems in relying on open-market operations and sales to keep the effective federal funds rate—the Fed's overnight policy rate—on target.

Under that precrisis arrangement, the Fed couldn't just buy assets willy-nilly. If it did, it would lose control of both the federal funds rate and the rate of inflation (Kroeger, McGowan, and Sarkar 2018). The workings of the Fed's corridor system thus supplied Fed officials with a powerful argument against attempts, whether by presidents, the Treasury, Congress, or special interest groups, to pressure the Fed to buy securities when it considered such purchases unnecessary. The connection between the size of the Fed's balance sheet and the economy's inflation rate thus served to buttress the Fed's otherwise fragile independence.

8

OPENING THE FLOODGATES

In October 2008, Fed officials unwittingly kicked that buttress away. In the wake of Lehman Brothers' September 15 failure, the Fed's emergency lending was causing the stock of bank reserves to grow rapidly. Fearing unwanted inflation and lacking sufficient System Open Market Account Treasury security holdings to continue sterilizing the Fed's lending operations as they had been doing, Fed officials sought, and were granted, permission to begin paying interest on bank reserves.[1] Their goal was to set a rate high enough to keep banks from placing excess reserves on the fed funds market. By paying such a rate while continuing to add to the supply of reserves, the Fed

---

[1] The Financial Services Regulatory Relief Act of 2006 would have permitted Federal Reserve Banks to start paying interest on depository institutions' reserve balances on October 1, 2011. The Emergency Economic Stabilization Act of 2008 changed the effective date to October 1, 2008. For further details concerning the reasons for these steps see Selgin (2018, 11–23).

inadvertently switched from its former, skewed corridor system to a floor system.

Once that switch occurred, the rate of interest on excess reserves (or IOER rate) became the Fed's chief monetary control instrument. For almost a decade, that rate also defined the upper limit of a new fed funds rate "target range."[2] The switch also meant that changes to the quantity of reserves, including changes due to open-market operations, would no longer influence the fed funds rate, other short-term interest rates, or broad measures of money and credit, even once the Fed's policy rate target was set well above zero. The Fed thus became able to resort to quantitative easing, not only as a desperate expedient during the recession, when rates were near their zero lower bound, but at other times as well. That is, it gained the power to buy large quantities of new assets and retain them indefinitely without sacrificing its ability to keep short-term interest rates at levels consistent with avoiding unwanted inflation. It's this power that proponents of fiscal QE would like to see the Fed and other central banks employ for non-macro-economic ends.

Oddly enough, some of these same fiscal QE proponents seem not to appreciate the greater scope for it provided by floor-type central bank operating frameworks. Thus Frances Coppola (2019, 88), referring specifically to possible drawbacks of helicopter money, observes

---

[2] The FOMC officially switched from a single-value fed funds rate target to a target range in December 2008 (Board of Governors 2008). Concerning the reasons for that change and subsequent changes in the relationship between the target range's upper limit and the IOER rate, see Selgin (2019a).

that "if the government . . . dictated to the central bank how much money to issue, the central bank would no longer have full control of base money creation" and would therefore "not be able to control inflation by itself." Although this would have been true under the pre-2008 Fed operating framework, and it continues to be so when central banks rely on corridor operating frameworks, it's no longer the case when central banks rely on adjustments to the rate of interest they pay on bank reserves, rather than to the size of their balance sheets, to regulate inflation.

A Free Parameter

As former Philadelphia Fed president Charles Plosser (2018, 8) observed several years back, by severing the link between the quantity of reserves the Fed creates and the level of short-term interest rates, a floor system "opens the door for Congress . . . to use [the Fed's] balance sheet for its own purposes." In other words, the size of the Fed's balance sheet becomes a "free parameter . . . ripe for misuse if not abuse."

> Congress would be free to lobby the Fed through political pressure or legislation to manage the portfolio for political ends. Imagine Congress proposing a new infrastructure bill where the Fed was expected, or even required, to buy designated development bonds to support and fund the initiative so taxes could be deferred. This would be very tempting for Congress. Indeed, in testimony before Congress I was asked why the Fed shouldn't contribute "its fair share" to an infrastructure initiative. Imagine the lobbying for the

Fed to purchase "build America bonds" issued by the Treasury to fund infrastructure initiatives.

Nor would Congress find it difficult to come up with other "appropriate" uses for the Fed's bond-buying powers if it could claim that those uses wouldn't interfere with the Fed's ability to conduct monetary policy. It might, for example, pressure the Fed to follow other central banks' lead by acquiring "green bonds" (Mutua 2019). Because the Fed's decision to switch to a floor system offered fiscal authorities a means for conducting credit allocation off-budget, it was, Plosser (2018, 8) says, "akin to opening Pandora's box."

The Fed's New Normal

Although the Fed at first resolved to close that box, it ultimately decided to leave it open. When the Fed began its first round of large-scale asset purchases at the start of 2009, Ben Bernanke said it would revert to its relatively lean balance sheet and precrisis methods of monetary control once the recession ended. But Fed officials later altered their "normalization" plans, choosing, among other things, to entertain the option of retaining its floor system of monetary control. At length, during his January 30, 2019, press conference Fed Chair Jerome Powell (2019, 3) announced:

> The [FOMC] made the fundamental decision today to continue indefinitely using our current operating procedure for implementing monetary policy. That is, we will continue to use our administered rates to control the policy rate with an ample supply of reserves so that active management of reserves is not required. This is often called a "floor system" or an "abundant reserves system."

Powell's announcement meant the Fed would retain its capacity to resort to quantitative easing even though interest rates had risen considerably above their zero lower bound. This meant that the Fed could make use of that capacity for nonemergency, if not non-macroeconomic, purposes.[3]

Some Fed officials themselves appeared to believe that quantitative easing might prove useful beyond the zero lower bound. Speaking around the time of Powell's announcement, San Francisco Fed President Mary Daly considered it "an important question" whether QE policies should "always be in the toolkit" (Smialek 2019a):

> Should you always have those at your ready, or should you think [of them as] tools you use when you really hit the zero lower bound and you have no other things you can do? . . . You could imagine executing policy with your interest rate as your primary tool, and the balance sheet as a secondary tool, but one that you would use more readily.

Daly was far from imagining, much less endorsing, the use of QE for purely fiscal purposes. Still, by choosing to keep a capacity for above-zero lower bound QE in its "toolkit" for *any* reason, the Fed made it possible for others to contemplate using the same tool for purely fiscal purposes.

---

[3] According to the most recently released FOMC transcripts, as of 2014 that committee was still divided then on the floor vs. corridor question, with roughly half of its members favoring a corridor. Although Powell, who was then Vice-Chair, preferred a floor system as offering "the best control over short-term rates at the lowest cost," he nonetheless recognized that the fact "that the size of the balance sheet is a matter of choice under a floor system" might cause that system to become "a magnet for trouble over time" (Board of Governors 2014, pp. 127-131).

9

FISCAL QE AS A FUNDING MECHANISM

Why shouldn't QE be used for purely fiscal purposes? Why not use it to fund government projects, such as those that make up the Green New Deal? If, thanks to its floor operating system, the Fed can go along with such plans without sacrificing control of inflation, why shouldn't it?

There are, as Frances Coppola (2019, 69) observes, several ways in which a central bank might employ QE to fund special government undertakings. It might acquire long-term government bonds issued by the central government itself, or ones issued either by existing government agencies or by a specially established state investment bank. Alternatively, it could buy the bonds of private corporations that take part in government spending initiatives.

The first of these options is the least controversial, so my criticisms will refer mainly to it.[1] But those criticisms

---

[1] Direct central bank investment in private-sector businesses is the most controversial option. As both Paul Tucker (2018, 483) and Frances Coppola (2019, 73) explain, it is so because a central bank that buys private securities is both assuming credit risk and steering credit toward particular economic sectors or borrowers.

apply with equal force to the other options as well, for in those cases the central bank is merely asked to do directly what the government might do indirectly using funds secured from large-scale central bank purchases of its own long-run securities.

Optimal Debt Structure

If one treats the Fed as part of the government, and then considers the government's consolidated balance sheet, it appears that there is no fundamental difference between Fed financing of government undertakings and financing funded by Treasury borrowing or taxation. Because the Fed can create bank reserves and issue circulating currency, however, its actions can alter the *structure* of the federal debt in ways Treasury actions alone can't mimic. For that reason, the possibility that fiscal QE might be uniquely able to contribute to an optimal overall government funding strategy can't be ruled out a priori.

When the Fed buys government bonds and replaces them with bank reserves, it reduces the length to maturity of outstanding privately held government debt. Doing that might achieve an optimal debt maturity structure that the Treasury alone can't achieve because its own short-term debt instruments are less useful to banks than interest-bearing reserves. John Cochrane (2012, 5–6) is among those who entertain this possibility. Treasury bills, he says,

> have awkward properties: They are only issued in large denominations, and they are rolled over frequently. The Treasury should go beyond bills, and issue floating-rate debt, held in electronic book-entry form.

> Either the Treasury can directly allow small denom-
> inations, or it can encourage money-market funds to
> intermediate for retail clients.
>
> The most "liquid" floating-rate debt has a constant
> principal value of $1.00, always. . . . Yes, this is
> interest-paying money, issued by the Treasury. Every
> collateral, liquidity, or money-like feature of one-
> month Treasury debt I can think of works better with
> such fixed-value floating-rate debt. Why bother [with]
> "money-like" monthly Treasuries, when we can have
> money itself, without suffering any interest cost?

To suggest that the Treasury *might* fund its debt more
efficiently by having the Fed swap reserves for its securities
is one thing; to show this to be a *likely* outcome is quite
another. To begin with, the "Ricardian Equivalence" the-
orem, made famous by Robert Barro (1974; 1979), suggests
that one debt maturity structure is as good as any other. If
Ricardian Equivalence holds, the Treasury isn't disadvan-
taged by its inability to issue overnight debt, and QE could
have no advantages over ordinary government borrowing.

But Ricardian Equivalence rests on several strong
assumptions that don't generally hold in the real world.[2]
To show that fiscal QE can be advantageous, one has to
identify one or more exceptions to those assumptions that
make the debt term structure matter, and then show that
the Treasury's existing instruments don't give it all the
flexibility it needs.

---

[2] These assumptions are that taxation creates no deadweight losses,
that government debt offers no liquidity services, and that capital markets are frictionless (Barro 1974).

Meeting this burden is not easy. Indeed, as Ben Bernanke's "works in practice but not in theory" quip suggested, even showing how *nonfiscal* QE can make a difference is far from easy. The most popular but nonetheless controversial explanation of how QE might prove beneficial—the "portfolio balance" theory—rests on the non-Ricardian assumption that debt markets are "segmented," with longer-term debt held mainly by specialized investors who insist on being compensated for bearing interest rate risk (Vayanos and Vila 2009). By swapping short-term reserves for long-term securities, the central bank assumes that risk, thereby permanently lowering long-term rates both absolutely and relative to short-term rates, compressing the term premium.

But the market segmentation that can make QE worthwhile as a venturesome gambit for reviving spending when rates reach their zero lower bound isn't necessarily worthwhile under ordinary circumstances. Other theories offered in defense of nonfiscal QE likewise supply no correspondingly compelling argument for its strictly fiscal counterpart.

Borrow Long, Invest Short

There is, however, a substantial literature, including Barro's seminal writings themselves, suggesting that, while the debt structure does indeed matter in the presence of interest-rate uncertainty and distortionary taxes, it does so in a manner *opposite* that which might favor fiscal QE. Under those conditions, Yves Nosbusch (2008, 477) explains:

> A benevolent government has an incentive to choose the composition of its debt portfolio in a way that allows it to achieve some degree of tax smoothing across states and

over time. The government can achieve such welfare-improving tax smoothing by issuing debt instruments that have the effect of partially expropriating debtholders in those states of the world that would otherwise require high tax rates.

In plain English, the government should "borrow long and invest short." The longer the duration of its debt, the more success the government will have in smoothing taxes despite various economic shocks (Nosbusch 2008, 497). The welfare gains from tax smoothing will generally suffice to justify the government's increased expected interest expense. Hanno Lustig, Christopher Sleet, and Sevin Yeltekin (2008) likewise show that reliance upon long-term debt minimizes the expected costs arising from distortionary taxes. It follows that a central bank that engages in quantitative easing for strictly fiscal purposes, replacing long-term Treasury securities with its own short-term obligations, is likely to make the public *worse* off by increasing expected tax distortions (Bassetto and Messer 2013, 430).

Fiscal QE as Fiscal Illusion

If fiscal QE is unlikely to be a welfare-enhancing way for the government to raise money, why would politicians ever call for it? The answer is twofold. First, fiscal QE may be attractive to them not because it's actually economically advantageous, but because it *appears* to be so. Specifically, fiscal QE may make the government programs it helps finance seem less expensive than they are, exploiting what public-choice theorists call "fiscal illusion"

(Oates 1985).[3] Second, by having the Fed directly finance their favored projects, legislators can steer clear of a congressional appropriations process that might prove those projects' undoing. In short, fiscal QE offers unprecedented opportunities to politicians seeking ways to fund "backdoor spending."

As we've seen, myopic politicians have long been tempted to exploit a central bank's lending powers even when doing so ultimately sponsors unwanted inflation. "Printing money" can be much easier than raising taxes, and less costly in the short run than competing with private-sector borrowers for credit. Also, the public may not fully grasp the connection between fiscal QE and any inflation that follows. Finally, shortsighted politicians, themselves unaware of quantitative easing's more subtle workings and consequences, might themselves suppose that by taking advantage of it to finance various projects, they really are providing the public with a "free lunch."

Fiscal QE lends itself to such misunderstanding and abuse because it looks to some like an opportunity for the government, or government-sponsored enterprises (GSEs), to borrow at favorable interest rates, if not interest-free. That's so in part because people familiar with the Fed's pre-2008 methods tend to assume that the Fed remits any interest earned on securities it purchases, net of its operating costs, to the U.S. Treasury. But in a floor system, that's

---

[3] More recently sociologist Sarah Quinn (2019) has referred to the political and fiscal "lightness" of certain credit-based means for funding government undertakings, meaning their ability to appear less burdensome than more direct financing, even when they are not so in fact.

not the case. Instead, much of the interest generated by the Fed's assets goes not to the Treasury but to banks, to reward them for holding excess reserves—that is, for lending to the Fed. Consequently, the government's funding cost actually consists of whatever rate the banks earn.

Furthermore, because the rate the Fed pays on bank reserves depends not on the yield from its security portfolio but on monetary policy considerations, the cost of funding the Fed's portfolio doesn't depend on the interest rate paid on the securities it purchases. To keep inflation at bay, for example, the Fed would generally have to pay interest on banks' excess reserves even if the securities it purchased yielded no interest at all, or if, instead of acquiring assets, it resorted to helicopter money.

Fiscal QE proposals often overlook these facts, giving readers the impression that selling zero-coupon perpetual bonds to finance government undertakings avoids the interest expense of those undertakings. Thus Coppola (2019, 70) observes, "If the central bank is wholly government owned," People's QE loans "could have an interest rate of zero, since this would really be a transfer between different parts of government." In fact, the fiscal outcome would be much the same as if the government auctioned short-term interest-bearing bills directly to the commercial banks funding the central bank's fiscal QE bond purchases.

In short, as Greg Ip (2019) observes, "the Fed can't make a Green New Deal cheaper without compromising its control of interest rates and thus inflation." What the Fed *might* do, by allowing its QE powers to be taken advantage of for purely fiscal purposes, is make a Green

New Deal, or any other large-scale government program, *appear* cheap, without actually making it so.

And that is why fiscal QE is so dangerous: Economists understand, of course, that free lunches are few and far between; and those who think in terms of a consolidated Fed–Treasury balance sheet will be quick to recognize that fiscal QE is no exception. But the general public doesn't think in terms of consolidated balance sheets. And while politicians may or may not do so, they will in any case find big-ticket projects easier to sell to voters if they can point to supposedly cheap ways to pay for them. Such considerations can make fiscal QE politically appealing even when it is a far cry from sound fiscal policy.

QE and Backdoor Spending

The other reason for fiscal QE's political appeal is its ability to support "backdoor spending," meaning federal agency spending that bypasses the annual congressional appropriations process.[4] Even before the Fed acquired its present quantitative easing powers, it was understood to be capable of facilitating backdoor spending. J. Alfred Broaddus, Jr., and Marvin Goodfriend (2001, 13) write:

> A healthy democracy requires full public disclosure and discussion of the expenditure of public funds.

---

[4] "Some 84 percent of all federal spending in 2015 (and likely a higher percentage now) consists of what subcommittee chairman Rep. Gary Palmer calls 'backdoor spending' that Congress allows without providing explicit annual authority. In all, $3.2 trillion of the total federal budget that year of $3.8 trillion fell into this broad category" (Hillyer 2018).

> The congressional appropriations process enables Con-
> gress to evaluate competing budgetary programs and to
> establish priorities for the allocation of public resources.
> Hence the Fed—precisely because it is exempted from
> the appropriations process—should avoid, to the full-
> est extent possible, taking actions that can properly be
> regarded as within the province of fiscal policy and the
> fiscal authorities.

Thanks to its post-2008 QE powers, the Fed's ability to encroach upon "the province of fiscal policy," and thereby fund government undertakings independently of the congressional appropriations process, is now far greater than it was when Broaddus and Goodfriend wrote.

Substantive legislation might, for example, create a new program to be carried out by either an existing or a new agency, while also granting that agency "borrowing authority" for the purpose of funding the program. Borrowing authority normally allows agencies to sell securities either to the Treasury or directly to the public. But if granted in conjunction with a fiscal QE plan, it could instead mean having agencies sell securities to the Fed.[5] As Modern Monetary Theorists Scott Fullwiler

---

[5] Borrowing authority originated with the establishment of the Reconstruction Finance Corporation in 1932. As James Butkiewicz (2002) explains, in addition to the $500 million of capital provided to it by the U.S. Treasury, "the RFC was authorized to borrow an additional $1.5 billion from the Treasury. The Treasury, in turn, sold bonds to the public to fund the RFC. Over time, this borrowing authority was increased many-fold. Subsequently, the RFC was authorized to sell securities directly to the public to obtain funds." All told "the RFC borrowed $51.3 billion from the Treasury, and $3.1 billion from the public."

and Randall Wray (2010, 20) explain, when agencies borrow from the Fed rather than the Treasury, the appropriations process is all the more thoroughly bypassed: whereas Treasury lending must itself be approved by Congress, "the Fed does not face such a budgetary constraint—it can commit Uncle Sam to trillions of dollars of commitments without going to Congress." Furthermore, agency borrowing isn't itself subject to statutory debt limits.[6]

Backdoor spending appeals to advocates of large-scale, ongoing spending programs that would otherwise be difficult to fund initially and more vulnerable to future funding interruptions. In a compelling critique of backdoor spending from a constitutional perspective, Kate Stith (1988, 1381) explains that fiscal illusion comes into play here as well:

> Of course, the true ("opportunity") cost of any permanent, indefinite, or backdoor spending authority is no different from the cost of an annual appropriation. But . . . Congress may operate (as a matter of policy or of psychology) under the illusion that funding for the activity does not affect other budgetary decisions, and that the present Congress is neither responsible nor accountable for the program.

---

[6] Debts incurred by independently owned GSEs are entirely excluded from the federal debt. This remains the case for Fannie Mae and Freddie Mac despite their having supplied the U.S. Treasury with warrants to purchase 79.9 percent of their common stock upon going into conservatorship in September 2008. The 79.9 percent figure was quite deliberate: had it been 80 percent, the federal government would have been obliged to carry the GSEs' debts on its balance sheet.

What backdoor spending certainly does is make it less likely that Congress will effectively control government spending. To the extent that the executive branch can bypass the appropriations process, Stith observes, it alone

> defines the scope and character of the public sphere, especially in areas that inherently require significant executive discretion. Congress abdicates, rather than exercises, its power of the purse if it creates permanent or other open-ended spending authority that effectively escapes periodic legislative review and limitation. (Stith 1988, 1345)

To their credit, Modern Monetary Theorists see little virtue in backdoor spending (or the "political lightening") of expensive government programs such as the Green New Deal. In an op-ed warning against attempts to mask the "burden of the GND on government balance sheets" by resorting to off-budget financing, Nathan Tankus, Andrés Bernal, and Raúl Carrillo (2019) insist that, if a program is considered "necessary for the collective good . . . *Congress should appropriate* as much public money as necessary" to pay for it (emphasis added). Thus, the MMT view that the Fed is bound to supply the government with all the money the government needs to fund whatever level of spending it chooses is not itself an argument for having the Fed directly fund particular government programs.

10

ADVERSE EFFECTS OF FISCAL QE

Although fiscal QE is unlikely to offer any genuine economic advantages, its potential costs could be substantial. As already noted, these costs are likely to include less-than-optimal tax smoothing, a corresponding increase in taxpayers' risk exposure, and reduced congressional control over federal spending.

While QE1 was still underway, Narayana Kocherlakota (2010), then-president of the Minneapolis Fed, explained:

> The Fed cannot literally eliminate the exposure of the economy to the risk of fluctuations in the real interest rate. It can only *shift* that risk among people in the economy. So, where did that risk go when the Fed bought the long-term bond? The answer is to taxpayers. . . . Basically, if the government uses short-term debt, it exposes taxpayers to interest rate risk. If it uses long-term government debt, it exposes the bondholders to interest rate risk. QE is a special case of this general principle: When the Fed buys long-term government debt from the private market, it shifts interest rate risk from bondholders to taxpayers.

Kocherlakota went on to say that, in theoretical models in which there is only a "representative" agent, this means nothing more than "shifting risk from one pocket [of the agent] to another." In reality, though, when the Fed swaps fresh reserves for long-term Treasuries, it shifts risk from the former holders of those securities to taxpayers.

Effects on the Fed's Earnings and Capital

Taxpayers aren't the only ones who bear extra risk when the Fed resorts to QE. By holding large quantities of long-term debt, the Fed involves itself in what Marvin Goodfriend (2014a, 2) refers to as a "bond market carry trade," with its own attendant risks. In particular, as Christopher Sims (2016, 13) explains, "a central bank with long-duration assets and short-duration liabilities (for example, interest-bearing reserves) will usually reduce its net worth by raising interest rates." Yet, because fiscal QE is expansionary the Fed must eventually raise rates to contain inflation, or else higher inflation will expose it to still larger losses (Goodfriend 2014a, 10). For obvious reasons, if QE took the form of "helicopter money" rather than central bank purchases of long-term government debt, the risk of loss would be especially great.

The Fed's accounting practices don't allow it to report negative undistributed net income. Instead, it must draw on its surplus capital to make up for losses, while suspending transfers to the Treasury in order to eventually replenish its surplus. "It is not difficult," Goodfriend (2014a, 12) observes, "to imagine circumstances in which a deeply negative net interest margin on the back end of a monetary carry trade could produce a negative cash flow problem," making it necessary for the Fed to dip into its (now meager) surplus capital to finance interest payments on bank reserves (Goodfriend 2014a, 19). Because the FAST Act also limits the Fed's ability to increase its surplus, if the Fed's losses become large enough, such negative cash flows might end up entirely depleting its capital.[1]

Although it's true that central banks can operate with no or even negative capital, as conventionally defined, that's so only because they can always cover their losses by creating more base money. Alternatively, those paying interest on bank reserves might reduce their losses by reducing those interest payments. However, central banks cannot generally take such steps without risking exceeding their inflation targets (Stella 1997; Archer and

---

[1] The Fed does have the option of making a call on member banks for any part of the 3 percent of their own capital that they are required to keep on reserve. Note, however, that even when it still had the power to do so, the Fed failed to set aside additional capital to cover itself from risks stemming from its large-scale purchases of long-term securities. See Goodfriend (2014a).

Were the Fed not able to carry unrealized losses on its balance sheet for an extended period of time, such losses would already have exhausted its capital. In December 2018, for example, the Fed reported unrealized losses of $66 billion—a value equal to 170 percent of its capital at the time—leaving it with marked-to-market net worth of *minus* $27 billion (Pollock 2019).

In the Fed's case, operating losses do not lead at once to any corresponding reduction in the Fed's capital surplus, but are instead capitalized as a "deferred asset"—a sort of Treasury IOU—that the Fed resolves by suspending remittances to the Treasury until it has made up its loss. The Fed's capital can nevertheless be depleted if for any reason its retained earnings fall short of its operating expenses.

Moser-Boehm 2013).[2] In the helpful terminology of Peter Stella and Åke Lönnberg (2008, 9ff), a central bank whose own resources might forever keep it technically solvent still risks becoming "policy insolvent." For that reason, a Fed bereft of capital, but determined to avoid exceeding its inflation target, might be obliged to seek a capital injection from Congress. Doing so could, in turn, undermine its independence if Congress asks for concessions in return for the injections. Alternatively, as Ulrich Bindseil, Andres Manzanares, and Benedict Weller (2004, 27) explain, to avoid any direct loss of its privileges the Fed might become "more pliable towards the Government" (see also Bassetto and Messer [2013, 429ff]).

Financial Instability

Despite tending to shift the risk burden associated with long-term securities from persons who might otherwise hold those securities to taxpayers and the Fed, quantitative easing can have "side effects that might endanger financial stability" (Dell'Ariccia, Rabanal, and Sandri 2018, 152). While these side effects may be of secondary importance in an economy struggling to escape from a recession, they can't be so easily overlooked when quantitative easing is meant to serve only fiscal ends.

---

[2] Although a central bank operating a floor system might acquire additional interest-earning assets without fueling inflation, it cannot generally count on making up losses that way, because the higher-yielding assets would likely also be risky. In the present context such purchases would amount to a "hair of the dog" remedy that could ultimately expose the central bank to further losses.

For example, the reduction of long-term risk premiums that's meant to stimulate investment also means a flatter yield curve and corresponding pressure on bank profits (Borio, Gambacorta, and Hofmann 2015; Borio and Gambacorta 2017). Banks are, after all, in the business of using short-term liabilities such as deposits and commercial paper to finance longer-term assets such as mortgages, asset-backed securities, and commercial loans. Their profitability depends directly upon the size of term premiums.

By reducing yields on relatively safe assets, quantitative easing can encourage some financial intermediaries to "reach for yield," turning to riskier alternatives in an effort to maintain their returns (Halton 2013). That temptation is greatest for pension funds and life insurance companies that have long-term liabilities promising definite yields (Rajan 2005). Here again, although the extra risk taking may have macroeconomic benefits in a recession, it's unlikely to be welfare-enhancing otherwise (Chodorow-Reich 2014).

Even during the 2007–2009 recession, some Fed officials worried about the risk taking that QE might encourage. Speaking at the FOMC's October 2012 meeting, soon after the Fed had begun its third and final round of quantitative easing, then-Governor Powell expressed his belief that the Fed had reached

> a point of encouraging risk-taking, and that should give us pause. Investors really do understand now that we will be there to prevent serious losses. It is not that it is easy for them to make money but that they have every incentive to take more risk, and they are doing so. Meanwhile, we look like we are blowing a

fixed-income duration bubble right across the credit spectrum that will result in big losses when rates come up down the road. You can almost say that that is our strategy. (Board of Governors 2012, 193)

Somewhat later Ben Bernanke (2013, 9) expressed similar concerns in testifying before the Joint Economic Committee:

Another cost—one that we take very seriously—is the possibility that very low interest rates if maintained for too long could undermine financial stability. For example, investors or portfolio managers, dissatisfied with low returns, may "reach for yield" by taking on more credit risk, duration risk, or leverage.

A 2017 International Monetary Fund study (Cecchetti, Mancini-Griffoli, and Narita 2017) of the effects of quantitative easing in the United States and elsewhere, based on data from a large number of bank and nonbank financial intermediaries, suggests that Fed officials' fears weren't misplaced. According to the study, QE contributed to a significant increase in financial risk taking, including increased leverage ratios. The study also found that "prolonged Federal Reserve policy easing leads banks and nonbanks *outside the U.S.* to take on more risks, with an effect similar to equivalent domestic monetary policies." (Cecchetti, Mancini-Griffoli, and Narita 2017, 22; emphasis added)

Harvard's Jeremy Stein (2018) concurs that increased risk taking goes hand-in-hand with quantitative easing. He observes:

This is not in itself a bad thing—it is just how monetary policy works. If one does not take some such risk when the unemployment rate is at, say, 8%, then one is probably not trying hard enough. So "excessive" completely depends on the context, and the relevant tradeoffs. By contrast, if we were at full employment and (counter-factually) inflation was stubbornly stuck at 1.5%, a hyper-aggressive monetary policy that disregarded financial risks, in a single-minded effort to return inflation to 2.0%, might well be said to be creating excessive financial risk.

If the extra risk taking that QE invites may make it not worthwhile even when the Fed is struggling to meet its mandate, then resorting to QE for strictly fiscal purposes hardly seems justifiable.

11

FISCAL QE, FULL EMPLOYMENT, AND INFLATION

Fiscal QE, in its strict sense, is QE that a central bank resorts to even though its policy rate can still be set at a level consistent with full employment. Provided the policy rate is indeed set in accordance with that goal, fiscal QE can't contribute toward the achievement of full employment. Instead, it only allows the government to employ resources that would otherwise be employed by the private sector.

In contrast, when there are unemployed resources, fiscal QE—like its nonfiscal counterpart—can promote fuller employment. But in that case, if rates are not at their lower bounds, a reduced policy rate is generally more effective and less dangerous. The same goes for combating below-target inflation. For these reasons, strictly fiscal QE can't easily be justified on strictly macroeconomic grounds.

Some Green New Deal proponents insist nonetheless on treating fiscal QE not simply as a supposedly economical way to finance their proposed programs, but as one that will bring substantial gains in employment. Such gains are possible, they say, because despite low official unemployment rates, the U.S. economy still harbors substantial unemployed resources, and Fed officials haven't been willing to lower their rate settings enough to absorb the slack.[1]

Greg Ip (2019) offers a thoughtful reply to this claim, which seems worth quoting in full. What some Green New Dealers claim, he says, "isn't impossible; unemployment has already fallen lower and employment grown faster than many economists thought possible without triggering inflation." In view of the likely scale of GND spending, Ip is granting a lot. Even so, he concludes that massive fiscal QE would be both unnecessary and risky. It's unnecessary, he says, because, in fine-tuning its policy rate settings, "the Fed is already probing how low unemployment can drop without spurring inflation." That is, the Fed is able, as we've already concluded, to rely on conventional rather than unconventional policy to combat unemployment. And fiscal QE is risky, not just because it exposes the Fed to potential losses, limits bank profits, and encourages long-term investors to reach for yield, but "because if inflation does take off, so will interest rates, and all that Green New Deal debt will start to snowball."

But suppose the Fed doesn't take steps to stem inflation. Suppose it's "pressured not to raise rates," when it ought to. In that case, Ip says (drawing upon an interview

---

[1] The Green New Deal's advocates claim it will also lead to substantial improvements in factor productivity. But that is a purported benefit of the spending itself, however it is financed, rather than of fiscal QE as such.

with George Washington University political scientist Sarah Binder), the consequences could be still worse:

> It wasn't purchases of housing debt in the 1960s and 1970s that sent inflation up, says Ms. Binder, but a "whole range of political pressures on the Fed to keep down rates from Lyndon Johnson continuing through Richard Nixon." Will some future president similarly feel that inflation should be subordinated to remaking society through a Green New Deal?

The possibility Ip raises shouldn't be dismissed. If the Fed doesn't raise the interest rate on reserves enough to avoid unwanted inflation, and the fiscal authorities don't themselves take steps to contain it, the Treasury enjoys short-run fiscal gains, as is typically the case with inflationary finance. Political myopia and "fiscal illusion" once again come into play. But as Claudio Borio (2016) has observed, in a slightly different context, the government's gains would come "at the cost of losing the public's confidence in our monetary institutions—a trust so painfully gained over the years—and with unpredictable consequences. It would be a Pyrrhic victory."

12

GUARDING AGAINST FISCAL QE

What can be done to keep the Fed from engaging in fiscal QE, or to at least limit the odds that it might do so? And who can do it? To answer the last question first, some suggested steps require cooperation between either Congress or the Treasury and the Fed, while others can be taken by either Congress or the Fed acting alone. First I'll consider several solutions calling for cooperation between the Fed and other parts of government. Then I'll consider steps that either Congress or the Fed might take unilaterally.

A New Treasury-Fed Accord

One way to guard against fiscal QE is to have the Fed and the Treasury negotiate a new accord aimed specifically at securing the Fed's right not just to choose its policy rate settings, but to determine the amount and composition of its asset holdings. Long before the advent of quantitative easing, Marvin Goodfriend (1994) proposed such an accord, with the aim of preventing the Fed from engaging in any sort of "credit" policy, by which he meant either long-term lending or purchases of assets other than Treasury securities (see also Broaddus and Goodfriend [2001]; Goodfriend [2014b]). Besides ruling out Fed funding of "expenditures that ought to get explicit Congressional authorization" (Goodfriend 1994, 573), Goodfriend's proposed accord would also rule out Fed liquidity assistance to insolvent institutions and FAST Act–type transfers of Fed assets to the Treasury.

Considered as a means for ruling out fiscal QE, Goodfriend's plan is at once too restrictive and not restrictive enough. As Paul Tucker, who served as the Bank of England's Deputy Governor throughout much of the Great Recession, observes (2018, 487), denying the Fed the ability to acquire non-Treasury collateral could prevent it from lending not just to insolvent banks but to solvent ones rendered illiquid by the seizing up of money markets. More recent accord proposals, by Charles Plosser (2009) and James Nason and Plosser (2012), suggest a solution to this particular problem. Nason and Plosser (2012, 24–45) write:

> The Treasury and the Fed could negotiate and commit to an accord under which the Treasury could agree that during a financial crisis it would exchange its own securities for non-Treasury securities purchased and held by the Fed, say, after 120 days. With such an accord, fiscal policy remains outside the province of the Fed, but policy has the flexibility to respond to a crisis in the short run.

As Plosser (2009, 4) says, such an agreement "would preserve the Fed's independence to control its balance sheet and ensure that the full authority and responsibility for fiscal matters remained with the Treasury and Congress, where it rightfully belongs."

Goodfriend's original plan is not restrictive enough in that it would not rule out fiscal QE operations involving either purchases of long-term Treasury securities or "helicopter money." Taking what seems the next logical step, Charles Calomiris (2014) suggests that the Fed cease to purchase long-term Treasury securities, reverting to the (Treasury) "bills only" policy it briefly instituted between 1958 and 1961:

> There is no need to abandon a "bills only" policy of buying Treasury bills to accomplish this growth in the money supply, so long as an adequate supply of bills is available in the market. Given that other asset purchases would entail fiscal as well as monetary policy actions by the central bank, a "pure" monetary policy is best accomplished through growth of bills, if the central bank's mission is confined to monetary policy (as in a democracy such as the United States, where Congress and the Executive are responsible for making fiscal decisions, such as purchasing MBS or other assets issued by the private sector). (Calomiris 2014, 5)

Whether a "bills only" policy would exclude helicopter money is by no means evident. What's certain is that it would rule out not just fiscal QE, but QE of any sort. The Fed would then be deprived of what many, rightly or wrongly, consider to be one of its only options for combatting recessions when short-term interest rates are at their effective lower bound (Tucker 2018, 485).

Here again, a modification akin to that proposed by Nason and Plosser could help: The Fed might take part in an accord allowing it to purchase and hold long-term Treasury securities only when short-term interest rates are at or very close to their lower bound. The Treasury could in turn agree to swap Treasury bills for those longer-term Treasury securities once rates recover. A "bills only" limitation to the Fed's permanent asset holdings would reduce the short-run appeal of fiscal QE while also substantially reducing its longer-term risks (Bassetto and Messer 2013; Ireland 2019, 333).[1]

Revising the Federal Reserve Act

Congress could in turn attempt to guard against fiscal QE by supplementing or revising the Federal Reserve Act. It could do so by providing the Fed with what Paul Tucker (2018, 488) calls a "fiscal shield," while specifying what he calls a "fiscal carve out." The fiscal shield would preserve the Fed's integrity by placing explicit limits upon "requests-cum-demands from government for monetary financing." The fiscal carve out would in turn specify strict criteria that securities must meet for the Fed to buy or lend against them. Unlike proposals for a new Treasury-Fed Accord, Tucker's proposal calls not for a negotiated agreement, but for "primary legislation," presumably meaning a revision of the Federal Reserve Act.

As a means for ruling out fiscal QE, Tucker's proposed reform has two drawbacks. First, although the fiscal shield is supposed to prevent the government from being

---

[1] As Bassetto and Messer (2013, 431) explain, so long as a central bank's excess reserves are invested in short-term bills, it need never suffer losses on its balance sheet.

able to demand monetary financing of its undertakings, the proposal exempts requests made "via a legislative act." Second, the fiscal carve out is vulnerable to the same criticism often leveled against the suggestion that Congress should compel the Fed to follow a monetary policy rule: If a monetary rule is defined too precisely, it may deprive the Fed of flexibility to respond appropriately to extraordinary circumstances. If the rule is vague, it may not place any meaningful limit on the Fed's powers. In the same way, too strict a fiscal carve out, listing those assets the Fed might purchase, could hamper its ability to address certain emergencies; too loose a fiscal carve out, giving only broad criteria that Fed assets must satisfy, might not suffice to keep fiscal authorities from abusing the Fed's balance sheet.

An Emergency Fiscal Authority

What we've called "quasi-fiscal" QE, and helicopter money in particular, may prove essential to combating future downturns. But Stanley Fischer and his BlackRock Investment Institute coauthors (Bartsch and others 2019, 10) recognize that such a policy constitutes a "slippery slope." It could lead to a situation in which central banks' "overall monetary policy stance is dominated by short-term political considerations" and to "uncontrolled fiscal spending" by way of MMT-style arguments to the effect that "there is only a tenuous link between inflation and money-financed deficits."

To avoid the threat to central bank independence that such a subordination of monetary to fiscal policy would entail, these authors propose that central banks establish a "standing emergency fiscal facility" (SEFF). The facility would be allowed to operate only "when interest rates cannot be lowered and a significant inflation miss is expected" and expressly charged with getting that rate back on target (Bartsch and others 2019, 11). Central bank authorities alone would determine the scale of SEFF operations. In the Fed's particular case, "Congress could create a special Treasury account at the Fed and authorize the FOMC to fill the account up to a pre-set limit" (Bartsch and others 2019, 12).

> Our proposal is for an unusual coordination of fiscal and monetary policy that is limited to an unusual situation—a liquidity trap—with a predefined exit point and an explicit inflation objective. Quasi-fiscal credit easing, such as central bank purchases of private assets, could be operated by the SEFF rather than the central bank alone to separate monetary and fiscal decisions. (Bartsch and others 2019, 11)

Although the BlackRock solution seems appealing, it raises a question: If under existing arrangements the government might abuse the Fed's powers of quantitative easing for strictly fiscal purposes, what is to keep it from abusing the SEFF? What guarantee is there, in other words, that the SEFF will itself remain entirely under the Fed's control? So far as the BlackRock proposal indicates, the only difference between the SEFF balance and the Treasury's TGA balance is that the FOMC is *not* allowed to directly fund the latter. The SEFF plan, then, may only serve to make an already slippery slope all the slicker. Rather than clarifying a blurred boundary line between monetary and fiscal policy, as its proponents hope, a SEFF could instead end up smudging that line even more.

Amending or Clarifying the 2006 Financial
Services Regulatory Relief Act

Congress could prevent the Fed from resorting to *strictly* fiscal QE without amending the Federal Reserve Act by repealing that portion of the 2006 Financial Services Regulatory Relief Act granting the Fed the power to pay interest on bank reserves. Depriving the Fed of that power would compel it to revert to its pre-2008 operating system, or something similar, thereby ruling out noninflationary quantitative easing, except when the Fed's policy rate is at its zero lower bound. Alternatively, Congress could amend the 2006 act to prevent the Fed from paying interest on banks' *excess* reserves, while allowing it to go on paying interest on their required reserve balances. This less Draconian option would be in keeping with the spirit of the interest-on-reserves provision of the 2006 act, the purpose of which was not to allow the Fed to operate a floor system but simply to eliminate the implicit reserve-requirement "tax" on bank reserves.

Finally, Congress could achieve a similar outcome by merely *clarifying* the 2006 act without otherwise amending it. As written, the act allows the Fed to pay interest on reserves at rates "not to exceed the general level of short-term interest rates." However, it does not refer to any specific short-term rates. The Fed was therefore left to specify the rates it might refer to, which it formally did in drafting its final rules for implementing the statute by including its primary credit rate among the short-term rates to be considered.

Because the Fed's primary credit rate is set well above the Fed's short-term rate target, and hence well above ınost other overnight rates, that maneuver has allowed the Fed to operate a floor system, while still being able to claim that it is abiding by the statute. This would not be possible were the statute clarified. For example, Congress might only allow the Fed to pay interest on reserves at rates "not to exceed Secured Overnight Financing Rate (SOFR)," a "broad measure of the cost of borrowing cash overnight collateralized by Treasury securities" developed by the Federal Reserve Bank of New York (Federal Reserve Bank of New York, n.d.).[2]

The Need for Unilateral Fed Action

Congress and the executive branch, alone or working together with the Fed, might well take steps to reduce the risk of fiscal QE. But at least three good reasons argue for unilateral Fed action—that is, for the Fed to take steps to guard against abuse of its balance sheet without depending upon Congress.

First and most obviously, some members of Congress, and some future administration, may see merit in fiscal QE, in which case they'd be unwilling or at least reluctant to favor any measure designed to preclude it. Second, whatever one Congress or administration might do, another can undo: steps taken by a predominantly anti-fiscal QE government today might be reversed by a predominantly pro-fiscal QE government of some future date. Finally, even if they would rather not have the Fed take part in any fiscal QE program, Fed officials are bound to resent,

---

[2] Alternatively, as discussed below, the Fed itself can amend its final rule implementing the act.

if not actively oppose, any attempt by the government to limit or otherwise interfere with the Fed's monetary control or emergency lending capabilities. Such interference would represent no less a challenge to the Fed's independence than legislation compelling it to take part in fiscal QE might.

For all of these reasons, it's desirable, if not crucial, that the Fed take responsibility for protecting itself—and the public—from a future fiscal QE onslaught.

A Corridor Framework

As we've seen, a new Treasury-Fed Accord might offer both the Fed and the public considerable protection against abuse of the Fed's balance sheet for purely fiscal ends, as well as risks stemming from such abuse. However, it would not entirely rule out such abuse. Moreover, a new accord would suffer the major drawback of requiring the Treasury's cooperation.

Fortunately, the Fed can take other steps to guard against abuse of its balance sheet—steps that call for relatively little cooperation from either the executive branch or Congress: It can modify its operating framework by replacing its present floor system with a corridor system. Instead of trying to guard against fiscal QE by limiting the *types* of assets the Fed can hold (as a new Treasury-Fed Accord might), a corridor system reform would guard against fiscal QE by constraining the *size* of the Fed's balance sheet (Plosser 2011, 4).

As has been noted, fiscal QE is possible only because the Fed's floor system allows it to resort to QE without losing control of inflation, even when interest rates are well above zero. The risk that politicians will try to exploit that possibility is all the greater now that the Fed has undertaken three massive rounds of quantitative easing without unleashing inflation. Now that the Fed has begun a fourth round of asset purchases, despite facing no immediate zero lower bound problem, politicians may be further emboldened.

By switching from its current floor system to a corridor system, the Fed would revive the pre-2008 connection between the quantity of assets it acquires and the stance of monetary policy. Large-scale Fed asset purchases would create excess reserves that, instead of being accumulated by banks, would be lent on the fed funds markets, driving the fed funds rate below target. The Fed could for that reason no longer engage in fiscal QE without sacrificing its control of inflation. Requests for it to engage in fiscal QE would therefore be tantamount to government interference with monetary policy.

Yet, by adopting a corridor system, the Fed would *not* sacrifice its ability to resort to nonfiscal quantitative easing whenever conventional expansionary monetary policy ceases to be effective. Setting aside the possibility of negative interest on reserves, conventional expansionary policy ceases to be effective only if both the targeted overnight rate and the interest rate on excess reserves fall to zero. When that happens, *a corridor system automatically becomes a floor system.*

Furthermore, the Fed has good reason for not wishing to resort to QE except when it has fully exhausted its capacity to lower short-term rates. According to Markus Brunnermeier and Yann Koby (2019), to the extent that it reduces banks' holdings of long-term bonds, QE can itself undermine the effectiveness of interest rate cuts in combating recessions, even causing such cuts to become contractionary rather than expansionary. In their terminology, QE tends to increase the "reversal interest rate." Once a central bank policy rate has fallen to that level, further cuts will reduce banks' net interest income enough to more than offset capital gains from maturity mismatching, discouraging bank lending. "Consequently," Brunnermeier and Koby (2019, 2) argue, "QE should only be employed after interest rate cuts are exhausted."

In short, quantitative easing remains possible in a corridor system when it may be macroeconomically necessary, and that is also when it's least likely to be counterproductive. On the other hand, it is not possible in a corridor system when it is both unnecessary and likely to be counterproductive. Thus, although a central bank that opts for a corridor system renounces strictly fiscal QE, it retains the ability to use QE whenever it may need to do so to achieve its monetary policy ends.[3]

---

[3] Were negative IOER possible, the Fed could maintain a corridor system even when overnight rates fall to zero. Whether conventional monetary policy remains effective in that case is an open question. Although bank reserves would carry an opportunity cost, banks might try to avoid it by hoarding paper currency rather than by lending more.

13

THE COSTS OF A CORRIDOR

A corridor system's relative immunity to fiscal abuse is only one of several considerations in deciding whether switching to a corridor system would be prudent. A general review of those other considerations falls beyond this study's scope. But a quick look at some of the more important concerns suggests that, setting fiscal considerations aside, there is no overwhelming reason why the Fed should prefer a floor to a corridor.

Banking System Liquidity

The chief advantage of a floor system, according to its champions, is that it allows the Fed to enhance banks' safety by equipping them with substantial quantities of liquid reserves (see, for example, Keister and McAndrews [2009]). But this argument isn't very compelling for several reasons. First, a large share of the excess reserves that the Fed has created since it adopted its floor system is held by branches of foreign banks that do no retail banking in the United States and are therefore exempt from FDIC premiums. The liquidity of such banks is obviously not very relevant to the stability of the U.S. banking system.

Second, Basel's Liquidity Coverage Ratio, to which U.S. banks have been subject since 2015, requires them to maintain substantial cushions of high-quality liquid assets (HQLAs) against their retail, and some wholesale, deposits. Although the Basel rules treat U.S. Treasury and agency securities as perfect substitutes for excess reserves, so long as those assets can be readily exchanged for reserves on the private market or, in emergencies, at the Fed, they are practically as liquid as reserves themselves. For this reason, although the Fed's floor system might once have allowed it to bolster what would otherwise have been an insufficiently liquid banking system, it is no longer needed for that purpose. Instead, a scarce-reserve corridor system can be made at least as liquid, and probably more liquid, than the present abundant-reserve system.

Simplified Monetary Control

Another advantage claimed for the Fed's floor system is that it simplifies the implementation of monetary policy by dispensing with any need for balance-sheet adjustments to keep interest rates on target. Instead of having to anticipate or respond to both changes in the demand for bank reserves and "autonomous" changes in their supply (as when the public deposits or withdraws currency) by engaging in offsetting open-market security sales or purchases, Fed officials merely have to set the Fed's own administered rates, including the IOER rate, at levels consistent with their rate targets.

But here again, the purported advantages of a floor system are not so great as they first appear. For various reasons, the effective fed funds rate, which the Fed continues to target, has been neither equal to the IOER rate nor related to it in an unchanging manner. Consequently, the Fed has had to resort to various expedients, including replacing its specific rate target with a rate target "range" and then adjusting—four times so far—the relationship between the IOER rate and that range's upper limit. In 2015, the Fed had to establish an overnight reverse repurchase (ON RRP) facility to enforce the range's lower limit. Finally, in mid-September 2019, when overnight rates surged above the Fed's target zone, it pumped additional reserves into the banking system to pull them down again, and has continued to do so, through both temporary and permanent open-market security purchases, ever since (Selgin 2019c). In short, under the Fed's floor system, keeping the fed funds rate on target, even after widening that target, has been anything but simple.

Nor need the challenge of using open-market operations to keep rates on target in a new Fed corridor system be substantially greater than it was before October 2008. It's true that several of the "autonomous" determinants of the supply of bank reserves, including movements of Fed deposit credits between commercial banks on the one hand and the accounts of the Treasury and foreign central banks on the other, have become considerably larger and more volatile since the switch (Logan 2017, 2018). Such volatility makes it much harder for Fed officials to anticipate those movements and adjust their open-market operations accordingly. But that's the case in large part because, after it switched to a floor system, the Fed no longer discouraged the Treasury and foreign central banks from making heavy use of their respective Fed facilities, the Treasury General Account, and the foreign repo pool.[1] If it adopts a corridor system, the Fed will once again have reason to limit the size and volatility of these nonreserve liabilities.

Moreover, there are many sorts of corridor systems, including ones with wider or narrower corridors, defined by the distance between the central bank's IOER or deposit rate and its emergency lending rate. The narrower the corridor, the less extensive the open-market operations required to keep the central bank's policy rate close to its target (Bindseil and Jabłecki 2011; Kroeger, McGowan, and Sarkar 2018, 2, 17–18). The Bank of Canada, for example, confines its policy rate to a corridor that's just 50 basis points wide. Too often, Paul Tucker (in Quarles 2019, 179-84) complains, Fed officials opposed to switching to a corridor system present the choice as one between a pristine floor system on the one hand and a pre-2008 Fed style corridor system on the other. The latter system did indeed make it necessary for the Fed to forecast the demand for bank reserves with great accuracy, and to undertake frequent open-market operations. But these aren't requirements of corridor systems as such. On the contrary: it is perfectly possible to design a corridor system that doesn't call for *any* forcasting of reserve demand or open-market operations.

---

[1] See Selgin (2019d). As Kroeger, McGowan, and Sarkar (2018, 47–48) explain, before October 2008 the Treasury would shift funds from the TGA to Treasury Tax and Loan accounts at commercial banks for the express purpose of limiting the day-to-day volatility of its TGA balance, and hence of the total outstanding quantity of bank reserves.

An Active Interbank Market

Provided its rate range isn't extremely narrow, a corridor system also has at least one distinct advantage over a floor system apart from that of limiting opportunities for balance-sheet abuse: by compelling banks to make do with few, if any, excess reserves, it promotes routine unsecured overnight lending and borrowing of such reserves.

By switching to a corridor system, the Fed would revive interbank lending on the fed funds market. And because such lending is unsecured, banks routinely taking part in it would once again have reason, as they did until the crisis, to stay informed about the safety of potential counterparties in that market (Furfine 2001). The result will be more consistent bank-to-bank monitoring and a correspondingly reduced risk of panic-based crises. According to Ulrich Bindseil (2016, 16), the long-term interbank lending relationships that tend to develop as a counterpart of routine interbank monitoring can help to support financial stability by allowing fundamentally sound banks to turn to the interbank market when they confront unexpected deposit outflows.[2] In fact, interbank lending is the "first resort" lending for which central bank lending is meant to be a backstop. By eroding the foundation for such lending, a floor system tends to convert any central bank that relies upon it for very long from a lender of last resort into a lender of *only* resort.

---

[2] The classic theoretical work on the role of active interbank lending and associated peer monitoring in limiting systemic risk is Rochet and Tirole (1996). For empirical evidence of the salutary effects of such monitoring see Furfine (2001) and Dinger and von Hagen (2009).

The Fed's post-2008 floor system has, in fact, all but eliminated interbank lending and borrowing on the fed funds market, giving banks that much less reason to keep tabs on and maintain long-term credit relationships with one another.[3] Whereas just before October 2008 the fed funds market witnessed about $200 billion daily in overnight loans, almost all of which were bank-to-bank, today's figure is about $70 billion. Furthermore, much of today's fed funds lending consists not of interbank lending, but of lending by the Federal Home Loan Banks and other GSEs to very large commercial banks, which allows the GSEs to gain indirect access to the interest on reserves balances to which banks alone are directly entitled.

Switching to a Corridor

Despite the Fed's recent decision to retain its floor system, at least some Fed officials understand that switching to a corridor system is still possible. Replying to criticisms of the Fed's floor system by Peter Fisher (2019), a former manager of the New York Fed's System Open Market Account, New York Fed Vice President Lorie Logan, who is now that account's manager, expressed her belief that the Fed "certainly could turn to" a corridor system, albeit one that "might improve [sic] some of the concerns we had with the precrisis system" (Fisher 2019, 254).

---

[3] On QE's adverse effect on interbank lending see Blasques, Brauning, and van Lelyveld (2018). The post-2008 collapse of interbank fed funds activity was not without precedent: the fed funds market also dried up during the Great Depression and World War II, when a combination of low interest rates and high perceived counterparty risk caused banks to hoard reserves (Balles et al. 1959, 29–30).

Although switching to a corridor isn't impossible, that doesn't mean it will be easy. On the contrary, it will take considerable preparation and planning. Because, as noted earlier, a corridor system can work well only if the stock of bank reserves remains largely under the Fed's control, the necessary preparations should include a strategy for limiting the Treasury's use of the Treasury General Account and foreign official institutions' use of the Fed's foreign repo pool. Elsewhere (Selgin 2019e) I've outlined specific steps the Fed might take toward these ends, along with some ways in which Congress might help.

A smoothly functioning corridor system also requires that excess reserves, instead of being locked up in a handful of large banks, flow freely to wherever they're most needed. To allow this, the Fed and other regulatory agencies will need to relax some current liquidity regulations, particularly the guidance they offer larger banks for implementing "living will" liquidity requirements: those requirements, as presently implemented, are the chief impediments to interbank reserve flows today (Baer, Court, and Nelson 2018). Although banks are nominally allowed to satisfy their liquidity requirements using not just excess reserves but other HQLAs, bank supervisors fear that, in a crisis, even such high-quality assets may prove difficult to liquidate. Consequently, they've encouraged large banks to favor reserves over other HQLAs in meeting certain liquidity requirements (Quarles 2019; Andolfatto and Ihrig 2019a).

To put supervisors' concerns to rest, the Fed should establish a fixed-rate full-allotment standing repo facility (SRF), as recommended by David Andolfatto and Jane Ihrig (2019a, 2019b). Fed officials are already considering such a facility as an alternative to ad hoc Fed repo market interventions for avoiding floor-system rate spikes (Cox 2019b; Derby 2019). But the same facility could also serve as a steppingstone toward, and crucial feature of, a new corridor system (Selgin 2019f). The SRF would establish and police the new corridor's upper limit or "ceiling." And by offering at all times to swap reserve credits for nonreserve HQLAs at a modest premium above the Fed's overnight rate target, it would also encourage bank supervisors to allow banks to satisfy their liquidity requirements, including resolution liquidity requirements, with safe securities rather than excess reserves.[4] Finally, were the Treasury and foreign official institutions given access to it, the SRF could help them limit their use of the TGA and foreign repo pool by making it safer for them to use nonreserve HQLAs to meet most of their own liquidity needs (Selgin 2019e). In these last-mentioned ways the SRF could significantly reduce the overall demand for Fed liabilities, making possible a correspondingly large reduction in the size of the Fed's balance sheet.

Once it has taken these steps, the Fed will be in a position to transition to a corridor. That means renewing the unwinding of the balance sheet that it began in

---

[4] Some Fed officials are concerned that banks taking advantage of the proposed SRF would suffer the same stigmatization that presently makes them unwilling to resort to discount-window loans. However, according to Bill Nelson (2019), this outcome is unlikely for several reasons. First, besides involving more counterparties, SRF operations would resemble once-routine Fed open-market purchases, which are stigma-free, rather than discount-window loans. Second, the SRF would accept only government securities, and perhaps only Treasury securities, as collateral.

October 2017 but abruptly ended in July 2019. Only this time the Fed would unwind with the deliberate aim of making reserves scarce again—scarce enough to revive routine interbank lending and borrowing in the secured repo market but also in the unsecured federal funds market. To keep the funds rate on target as reserves become scarce again, the Fed will have to set its IOER rate further *below* that target to encourage more banks with excess reserves to part with them. To minimize sudden "autonomous" changes to the supply of bank reserves, it should insist that the Treasury and foreign central banks manage their Fed accounts with that end in mind. And to limit those fed funds rate fluctuations within the corridor limits, it must once again forecast those autonomous changes in reserve supply and demand that can't be avoided and offset them with regular small-scale open-market operations.

Finally, for good measure, the Fed should consider rewriting its IOER final implementation rule, as given in Part 204 of Title 12 of the Code of Federal Regulations (12 CFR Part 204, 2015). The present rule states:

> For purposes of this section, "short-term interest rates" are rates on obligations with maturities of no more than one year, such as the primary credit rate and rates on term federal funds, term repurchase agreements, commercial paper, term Eurodollar deposits, and other similar instruments.

The listed rates in this passage have clearly been chosen to allow the Fed to maintain its floor system, which has in practice often called for an IOER rate *above* rather than at or below comparable market rates. The primary discount rate's presence on the list is particularly hard to account for otherwise. The Fed can put an end to this embarrassing legal legerdemain, while binding itself more firmly to a corridor system, by requesting that the paragraph above be rewritten to say:

> For purposes of this section, "short-term interest rates" are rates on overnight, risk-free obligations, such as the overnight effective federal funds rate and overnight repurchase agreements, as represented by the Federal Reserve Bank of New York's Secure Overnight Financing Rate (SOFR).

The SOFR, which was first published in August 2018, was originally intended to serve as a reference or benchmark interest rate in place of the discredited London Interbank Offered Rate (LIBOR). Because bank reserves are essentially secured overnight obligations, the SOFR is a logical representative of those "general" interest rates to which the IOER rate is most comparable.

14

CONCLUSION

The Fed's postcrisis operating framework exposes it to pressure to resort to "fiscal" quantitative easing, aimed not at combating recession but at financing government programs. Should the Fed be unable to resist such pressure, or should Congress pass legislation compelling it to undertake fiscal QE, the consequences are likely to prove harmful to both the general public and the Fed itself. And although Congress might take steps to guard against such future abuse of the Fed's quantitative easing powers, that solution is both less likely and less appealing than the alternative: which is for the Fed itself to rule out the possibility of fiscal QE by switching from its present "floor" operating framework to a symmetric corridor system.

REFERENCES

Abrams, B. A. 2006. "How Richard Nixon Pressured Arthur Burns: Evidence from the Nixon Tapes." *Journal of Economic Perspectives* 20, no. 4 (Fall): 177–88.

Akers, B., and M. Chingos. 2013. "Policymakers Get Serious about Student Loan Interest Rates." *Brookings.edu*, May 10.

Andolfatto, D., and J. Ihrig. 2019a. "Why the Fed Should Create a Standing Repo Facility." *On the Economy Blog*, Federal Reserve Bank of St. Louis, March 6.

————. 2019b. "The Fed and a Standing Repo Facility: A Follow-Up." *On the Economy Blog*, Federal Reserve Bank of St. Louis, April 19.

Andolfatto, D., and L. Li. 2013. "Is the Fed Monetizing Government Debt?" *Central Banker* 23, no. 1 (Spring): 8–10.

Archer, D., and P. Moser-Boehm. 2013. "Central Bank Finances." BIS Papers no. 71, Bank for International Settlements, Basel, Switzerland.

Baer, G., J. Court, and B. Nelson. 2018. "Rethinking Living Will Liquidity Requirements." *BPI Blog*. Bank Policy Institute, May 3.

Balles, J. J., N. N. Bowsher, H. Brandt, D. R. Cawthorne, G. M. Conkling, J. D. Daane, L. M. Dembitz, et al. 1959. *The Federal Funds Market: A Study by a Federal Reserve System Committee.* Washington: Federal Reserve Board of Governors, May.

Barro, R. J. 1974. "Are Government Bonds Net Wealth?" *Journal of Political Economy* 82, no. 6: 1095–117.

Barro, R. J. 1979. "On the Determination of the Public Debt." *Journal of Political Economy* 87, no. 5: 940–71.

Bartsch, E., J. Boivin, S. Fischer, and P. Hildebrand. 2019. "Dealing with the Next Downturn: From Unconventional Monetary Policy to Unprecedented Policy Coordination." *Macro and Market Perspectives*, BlackRock Investment Institute, August.

Bassetto, M., and T. Messer. 2013. "Fiscal Consequences of Paying Interest on Reserves." *Fiscal Studies* 34, no. 4 (December): 413–36.

Bernanke, B. 2011. "The Economic Outlook and Monetary and Fiscal Policy." Testimony before the House Committee on the Budget, 112th Cong., 1st sess., February 9.

———. 2013. "The Economic Outlook." Testimony before the Joint Economic Committee, 113th Cong., 1st sess., May 22.

———. 2014. Interview by Liaquat Ahamed. "Central Banking after the Great Recession: Lessons Learned and Challenges Ahead." Transcript excerpt. The Brookings Institution, January 16.

———. 2015. "Budgetary Sleight-of-Hand." *Ben Bernanke's Blog*. The Brookings Institution, November 9.

———. 2016. "What Tools Does the Fed Have Left? Part 3: Helicopter Money." *Ben Bernanke's Blog*. The Brookings Institution, April 11.

Bernoth, K., P. König, and C. Raab. 2015. "Large-Scale Asset Purchases by Central Banks II: Empirical Evidence." DIW Roundup: Politik im Focus no. 61, Deutsches Institut für Wirtschaftsforschung (German Institute for Economic Research), Berlin.

Binder, S., and M. Spindel. 2017. *The Myth of Independence: How Congress Governs the Federal Reserve.* Princeton, NJ: Princeton University Press.

Bindseil, U. 2016. "Evaluating Monetary Policy Operational Frameworks." Paper prepared for the Economic Policy Symposium, Jackson Hole, Wyoming, August 25–27.

Bindseil, U., and J. Jabłecki. 2011. "The Optimal Width of the Central Bank Standing Facilities Corridor and Banks' Day-to-Day Liquidity Management." ECB Working Paper Series no. 1350, European Central Bank, Frankfurt.

Bindseil, U., A. Manzanares, and B. Weller. 2004. "The Role of Central Bank Capital Revisited." ECB Working Paper Series no. 392, European Central Bank, Frankfurt.

Blasques, F., F. Bräuning, and I. van Lelyveld. 2018. "A Dynamic Network Model of the Unsecured Interbank Lending Market." *Journal of Economic Dynamics and Control* 90 (May): 310–42.

Board of Governors. 2008. "FOMC Statement." Press release, Federal Reserve System, December 16.

———. 2014. Transcript meeting of the Federal Open Market Committee, Federal Reserve System, Washington, October 23–24.

Borio, C. 2016. "Helicopter Money—Reality Bites." Speech. Bank of International Settlements, September 6.

Borio, C., and L. Gambacorta. 2017. "Monetary Policy and Bank Lending in a Low Interest Rate Environment: Diminishing Effectiveness?" *Journal of Macroeconomics* 54, part B (December): 217–31.

Borio, C., L. Gambacorta, and B. Hofmann. 2015. "The Influence of Monetary Policy on Bank Profitability." BIS Working Papers no. 514, Bank for International Settlements, Basel, Switzerland.

Broaddus, J. A., Jr., and M. Goodfriend. 2001. "What Assets Should the Federal Reserve Buy?" Federal Reserve Bank of Richmond *Economic Quarterly* 87, no. 1 (Winter): 7–22.

Brown, E. 2011. "QE4: Forgive the Students." *Radical Voice*, October 21.

———. 2013. "Elizabeth Warren's QE for Students." *Counter-Punch*, June 14.

Brunnermeier, M. K., and Y. Koby. 2019. "The Reversal Interest Rate." IMES Discussion Paper no. 2019-E-6, Institute for Monetary and Economic Strategy, Bank of Japan, Tokyo.

Bryan, M. 2013. "The Great Inflation: 1965–1982." Essay. Federal Reserve History, November 22.

Butkiewicz, J. 2002. "Reconstruction Finance Corporation." Entry. EH.Net Encyclopedia, Economic History Association, July 19.

Calomiris, C. 2014. "Making Central Banks More Resistant to Political Pressures and Fads." *Economics 21*, April 14.

Calvert Jump, R., R. Dowler, D. Elson, D. Gabor, S. Himmelweit, L. Kalisperas, M. Lloyd, O. Onaran, and A. Ross. 2017. "A National Investment Bank for Britain: Putting Dynamism into Our Industrial Strategy." Report to the Shadow Chancellor of the Exchequer and Shadow Secretary for Business, Energy and Industrial Strategy on Implementation, Labour Party, London.

Cecchetti, S. G., T. Mancini-Griffoli, and M. Narita. 2017. "Does Prolonged Monetary Policy Easing Increase Financial Vulnerability?" IMF Working Paper no. 17/65, International Monetary Fund, Washington, DC.

Chodorow-Reich, G. 2014. "The Employment Effects of Credit Market Disruptions: Firm-Level Evidence from the 2008–09 Financial Crisis." *Quarterly Journal of Economics* 129, no. 1 (February): 1–59.

Cochrane, J. H. 2012. "Having Your Cake and Eating It Too: The Maturity Structure of US Debt." *Chicago Booth* (website), November 15.

Cohen, P. 2019. "Modern Monetary Theory Finds an Embrace in an Unexpected Place: Wall Street." *New York Times*, April 5.

Condon, C. 2018. "Congress Raids Fed's Surplus for $2.5 Billion in Budget Deal." Bloomberg, February 9.

Conti-Brown, P. 2016. *The Power and Independence of the Federal Reserve*. Princeton, NJ: Princeton University Press.

Coppola, F. 2015. "Jeremy Corbyn's 'People's QE' Scheme Misses the Point." *Financial Times*, August 24.

———. 2019. *The Case for People's Quantitative Easing*. Medford, MA: Polity Press.

Cox, J. 2019a. "Powell Says Economic Theory of Unlimited Borrowing Supported by Ocasio-Cortez Is Just 'Wrong.'" CNBC, February 26.

———. 2019b. "The Fed Is Looking at a 'Standing Repo' Operation to Handle Overnight Funding Issues." CNBC, November 20.

Dell'Ariccia, G., P. Rabanal, and D. Sandri. 2018. "Unconventional Monetary Policies in the Euro Area, Japan, and the United Kingdom." *Journal of Economic Perspectives* 32, no. 4 (Fall): 147–72.

Derby, M. S. 2019. "Fed Officials Weighed Money-Market Control Strategies at October Meeting." *Wall Street Journal*, November 20.

Dinger, V. and J. von Hagen. 2009. "Does Interbank Borrowing Reduce Bank Risk?" *Journal of Money, Credit and Banking* 41, no. 2/3 (March-April): 491–506.

Elliot, L. 2015. "Is Jeremy Corbyn's Policy of 'Quantitative Easing for People' Feasible?" *The Guardian*, August 14.

Federal Reserve Bank of New York. (n.d.) "Secured Overnight Financing Rate Data."

Fessenden, H. 2015. "A Bridge Too Far?" Federal Reserve Bank of Richmond *Econ Focus*, Third Quarter: 4–7.

Fisher, P. 2019. "Should the Fed 'Stay Big' or 'Slim Down'?" In *Currencies, Capital, and Central Bank Balances*, ed. J. H. Cochrane, J. B. Taylor, and K. Palermo, 237–60. Stanford, CA: Stanford University Hoover Institution Press.

Foxwell, H. S. 1911. "Introduction." In *History of the Bank of England and Its Financial Services to the State*, by E. von Philippovich, 5–20. Washington: Government Printing Office.

Friedman, M. 1966. "Comments." In *Guidelines, Informal Controls, and the Market Place: Policy Choices in a Full Employment Economy*, ed. G. P. Shultz and R. Z. Aliber, 55–61. Chicago: University of Chicago Press.

———. 1969. "The Optimum Quantity of Money." In *The Optimum Quantity of Money and Other Essays*, 1–30. Chicago: University of Chicago Press.

Fullwiler, S., R. Grey, and N. Tankus. 2019. "An MMT Response on What Causes Inflation." *FT Alphaville*, March 1.

Fullwiler, S., S. Kelton, C. Ruetschlin, and B. Steinbaum. 2018. "The Macroeconomic Effects of Student Debt Cancellation." Research Project Reports, Levy Economics Institute of Bard College, New York, February.

Fullwiler, S., and R. L. Wray. 2010. "Quantitative Easing and Proposals for Reform of Monetary Policy Operations." Working Paper no. 645, Levy Economics Institute of Bard College, New York.

Furfine, C. H. 2001. "Banks as Monitors of Other Banks: Evidence from the Overnight Federal Funds Market." *Journal of Business* 74, no. 1: 33–57.

Gagnon, J. E. 2018. "QE Skeptics Overstate Their Case." Realtime Economic Issues Watch, Peterson Institute for International Economics, July 5.

Gagnon, J., M. Raskin, J. Remache, and B. Sack. 2011a. "The Financial Market Effects of the Federal Reserve's Large-Scale Asset Purchases." *International Journal of Central Banking* (March): 3–43.

———. 2011b. "Large-Scale Asset Purchases by the Federal Reserve: Did They Work?" Federal Reserve Bank of New York *Economic Policy Review* 17, no. 1: 41–59.

Goodfriend, M. 1994. "Why We Need an 'Accord' for Federal Reserve Credit Policy: A Note." *Journal of Money, Credit and Banking* 26, no. 3, part 2 (August): 572–80.

———. 2014a. "Monetary Policy as a Carry Trade." IMES Discussion Paper no. 2014-E-8, Institute for Monetary and Economic Studies, Bank of Japan, Tokyo.

———. 2014b. "The Case for a Treasury–Federal Reserve Accord for Credit Policy." Testimony before the Subcommittee on Monetary Policy and Trade of the House Committee on Financial Services, 113th Cong., 2nd sess., March 12.

Green New Deal Group. 2008. *A Green New Deal*. London: New Economics Foundation.

Greenlaw, D., J. D. Hamilton, E. Harris, and K. D. West. 2018. "A Skeptical View of the Impact of the Fed's Balance Sheet." NBER Working Paper no. 24687, National Bureau of Economic Research, Cambridge, MA, June.

The Guardian. 2018. "The *Guardian* View on QE: The Economy Needs More Than a Magic Money Tree." Editorial. April 15.

Halton, R. 2013. "Reaching for Yield." Federal Reserve Bank of Richmond *Econ Focus*, Third Quarter: 5–8.

Heller, R. 2016. "How Congress Gutted the Fed's Capital Coffers." *American Banker* (February 16).

Hetzel, R. L., and R. Leach. 2001. "The Treasury-Fed Accord: A New Narrative Account." Federal Reserve Bank of Richmond *Economic Quarterly* 87, no. 1 (Winter): 33–55.

Hillyer, Q. 2018. "Congress Should Stop Unchecked, Unmonitored 'Backdoor' Spending." *Washington Examiner*, December 16.

Ip, G. 2019. "Green New Deal Won't Enjoy a Free Lunch at the Fed." *Wall Street Journal*, February 20.

Ireland, P. N. 2019. "Interest on Reserves: History and Rationale, Complications and Risks." *Cato Journal* 39, no. 2 (Spring/Summer): 327–37.

Jill Stein for President. 2015a. "Stein/Baraka Campaign Debunks John Oliver's Deceptive Attack on Student Debt Bailout." Jill 2016 (website).

———. 2015b. "Student Debt Proposals." Jill 2016 (website).

Keister, T., and J. J. McAndrews. 2009. "Why Are Banks Holding So Many Excess Reserves?" Staff Reports no. 380, Federal Reserve Bank of New York, New York, July.

Kelton, S., A. Bernal, and G. Carlock. 2018. "We Can Pay for a Green New Deal." *Huffington Post*, November 30.

Kimball, M. 2016. "What Is the Effective Lower Bound on Interest Rates Made Of?" *Confessions of a Supply-Side Liberal Blog*, May 31.

Klein, M. C. 2015. "Corbyn's 'People's QE' Could Actually Be a Decent Idea." *Financial Times*, August 6.

Kocherlakota, N. 2010. "Economic Outlook and the Current Tools of Monetary Policy." Speech at the European Economics and Financial Centre, London, September 29.

Kroeger, A., J. McGowan, and A. Sarkar. 2018. "The Pre-Crisis Monetary Policy Implementation Framework." Federal Reserve Bank of New York *Economic Policy Review* 24, no. 2 (October): 38–70.

Lawler, J. 2015. "Fed Pushes Back against $30b Raid by Cash-Hungry Congress." *Washington Examiner*, November 9.

Liesse, A. 1909. *Evolution of Credit and Banks in France.* Washington: Government Printing Office.

Logan, L. K. 2017. "Implementing Monetary Policy: Perspective from the Open Market Trading Desk." Speech before the Money Marketeers of New York University, New York City, May 18.

———. 2018. "Operational Perspectives on Monetary Policy Implementation: Panel Remarks on 'The Future of the Central Bank Balance Sheet.'" Speech at the Policy Conference on Currencies, Capital, and Central Bank Balances, Hoover Institution, Stanford University, Stanford, CA, May 4.

Long, C. 2012. "Why the Federal Reserve Should Buy National Infrastructure Bonds." *Reuters*, December 28.

Lustig, H., C. Sleet, and S. Yeltekin. 2008. "Fiscal Hedging with Nominal Assets." *Journal of Monetary Economics* 55, no. 4: 710–27.

Mabie, B. 2012. "The Next Round of Quantitative Easing Should Be a Debt Jubilee." Economy & Growth, Roosevelt Institute, March 14.

Muellbauer, J. 2014. "Combatting Eurozone Deflation: QE for the People." *Vox*, December 23.

Mueller, F. W. 1952. "The Treasury-Federal Reserve Accord." *Journal of Finance* 7, no. 4 (December): 596–99.

Murphy, R., and C. Hines. 2010. "Green Quantitative Easing: Paying for the Economy We Need." Report. Finance for the Future, Norfolk, UK, December.

Mutua, D. C. 2019. "Green Bonds Might Soon Find Their Ultimate Buyer: Central Banks." Bloomberg, October 28.

Nason, J., and C. I. Plosser. 2012. "Time-Consistency and Credible Monetary Policy after the Crisis." Federal Reserve Bank of Philadelphia *Business Review*, Second Quarter: 19–26.

Nelson, B. 2019. "Design Challenges for a Standing Repo Facility." *BPI Blog*. Bank Policy Institute, August 13.

Nersisyan, Y., and L. R. Wray. 2019. "How to Pay for the Green New Deal." Working Paper no. 931, Levy Economics Institute of Bard College, New York.

New Economics Foundation. 2016. "An Economy for the People, by the People, about the New Economics Foundation." About Us. New Economics Foundation, London, October 6.

Nosbusch, Y. 2008. "Interest Costs and the Optimal Maturity Structure of Government Debt." *Economic Journal* 118, no. 527: 477–98.

Oates, W. E. 1985. *On the Nature and Measurement of Fiscal Illusion: A Survey*. College Park: University of Maryland Press.

Peterson, E. 2013. "Is Quantitative Easing an Option for Infrastructure Financing?" Article. Eno Center for Transportation, January 26.

Plosser, C. I. 2009. "Ensuring Sound Monetary Policy in the Aftermath of Crisis." Speech at the U.S. Monetary Policy Forum, The Initiative on Global Markets, University of Chicago Booth School of Business, New York, February 27.

———. 2011. "Exit." Speech before the Shadow Open Market Committee, New York, March 25.

———. 2012. "Fiscal Policy and Monetary Policy: Restoring the Boundaries." Speech at the U.S. Monetary Policy Forum, Initiative on Global Markets, University of Chicago Booth School of Business, New York, February 24.

———. 2018. "The Risks of a Fed Balance Sheet Unconstrained by Monetary Policy." In *The Structural Foundations of Monetary Policy*, ed. M. D. Bordo, J. H. Cochrane, and A. Seru, 1–16. Stanford, CA: Hoover Institution Press.

Pollock, A. J. 2019. "The Fed Is Technically Insolvent. Should Anybody Care?" *American Banker*, January 10.

Powell, J. 2019. Transcript of press conference, Federal Reserve System, January 30.

Quarles, R. K. 2019. "Liquidity Regulation and the Size of the Fed's Balance Sheet." In *Currencies, Capital, and Central Bank Balances*, ed. J. H. Cochrane, J. B. Taylor, and K. Palermo, 153–92. Stanford, CA: Hoover Institution Press.

Quinn, S. L. 2019. *American Bonds: How Credit Markets Shaped a Nation*. Princeton, NJ: Princeton University Press.

Rajan, R. G. 2005. "Has Financial Development Made the World Riskier?" NBER Working Paper no. 11728, National Bureau of Economic Research, Cambridge, MA.

Reichlin, L., A. Turner, and M. Woodford. 2019. "Helicopter Money as a Policy Option." *Vox*, September 23.

Reserve Requirements of Depository Institutions (Regulation D), Title 12, U.S. Code § 248, 3105, 461, 601, and 611.

Roberds, W., and F. R. Velde. 2014. "Early Public Banks." Working Paper no. 2014–03, Federal Reserve Bank of Chicago.

Rochet, J., and J. Tirole. 1996. "Interbank Lending and Systemic Risk." *Journal of Money, Credit and Banking* 28, no. 4, part 2 (November): 733–62.

Rogoff, K. 2019. "Modern Monetary Nonsense." *Project Syndicate*, March 4.

Romero, J. 2013. "Treasury-Fed Accord, March 1951." Essay. Federal Reserve History, November 22.

Ryan-Collins, R., R. Werner, T. Greenhorn, and G. Bernardo. 2013. "Strategic Quantitative Easing: Stimulating Investment to Rebalance the Economy." Report. New Economics Foundation, London.

Samuelson, R. J. 2008. *The Great Inflation and Its Aftermath: The Past and Future of American Affluence*. New York: Random House.

Selgin, G. 2016. "One Sentence, or, Unpacking the Truth about the Founding of the Bank of France." *Alt–M*, January 21.

_____. 2018. *Floored! How a Misguided Fed Experiment Deepened and Prolonged the Great Recession*. Washington: Cato Institute.

_____. 2019a. "Fed Watchers Should Keep an Eye on the IOER-SOFR Spread." *Alt-M*, July 25.

_____. 2019b. "On Empty Purses and MMT Rhetoric." *Alt-M*, March 5.

_____. 2019c. "Reflections on the Repo-Market Imbroglio." *Alt-M*, October 3.

_____. 2019d. "Stop the Presses! or, How the Fed Can Avoid Reserve Shortages without Bulking-Up, Part 1." *Alt-M*, November 12.

_____. 2019e. "Stop the Presses! or, How the Fed Can Avoid Reserve Shortages without Bulking-Up, Part 2." *Alt-M*, November 14.

_____. 2019f. "The Fed's New Repo Plan." *Alt-M*, May 2.

Sims, C. A. 2016. "Fiscal Policy, Monetary Policy and Central Bank Independence." Paper prepared for the Economic Policy Symposium, Jackson Hole, Wyoming, August 25–27.

Skidelsky, R. 2015. "Why We Should Take Corbynomics Seriously." *The Guardian*, August 19.

Smialek, J. 2019a. "Balance Sheet Could Be in Regular Fed Toolkit, Daly Suggests." Bloomberg, February 8.

_____. 2019b. "Fed Unveils Plan to Expand Balance Sheet but Insists It's Not Q.E." *New York Times*, October 11.

Smith, N. 2019. "The Green New Deal Would Spend the U.S. into Oblivion." Bloomberg Opinion, February 8.

Stein, J. 2018. "Have Low Interest Rates Led to Excessive Risk Taking?" American Economic Association Web Forum (comment on post).

Stella, P. 1997. "Do Central Banks Need Capital?" IMF Working Paper WP/97/83, International Monetary Fund, Washington, DC.

Stella, P., and Å. Lönnberg. 2008. "Issues in Central Bank Finance and Independence." IMF Working Paper WP/08/37, International Monetary Fund, Washington, DC.

Stith, K. 1988. "Congress' Power of the Purse." *Yale Law Journal* 97, no. 7 (June): 1343–96.

Tankus, N., A. Bernal, and R. Carrillo. 2019. "The Green New Deal Will Be Tremendously Expensive. Every Penny Should Go on the Government's Tab." *Business Insider*, September 23.

Thornton, D. L. 2015. "Requiem for QE." Cato Institute Policy Analysis no. 783, November 17.

Trump, D. (@realDonald Trump). 2019. ". . . up like a rocket . . ." Twitter post, April 30, 11:05 a.m. https://twitter.com/real DonaldTrump/status/1123287154833203200.

Tucker, P. 2018. *Unelected Power: The Quest for Legitimacy in Central Banking and the Regulatory State*. Princeton, NJ: Princeton University Press.

———. 2019. Discussant's remarks on R. K. Quarles, "Liquidity Regulation and the Size of the Fed's Balance Sheet." In *Currencies, Capital, and Central Bank Balances*, ed. J. H. Cochrane, J. B. Taylor, and K. Palermo, 170-85. Stanford, CA: Hoover Institution Press.

U.S. Congress, House. 2015. Fixing America's Surface Transportation Act (FAST Act), H.R. 22, 114th Cong., 1st sess., Public Law 114–94.

U.S. Congress, Senate. 2013. Bank on Students Loan Fairness Act, S. 897, 113th Cong., 1st sess., May 8.

———. 2019. Joint Resolution Recognizing the Duty of the Federal Government to Create a Green New Deal, S.J. Res. 8, 116th Cong., 1st sess., February 13.

U.S. Department of Transportation. (n.d.) "Private Activity Bonds."

Vayanos, D., and J. Vila. 2009. "A Preferred-Habitat Model of the Term Structure of Interest Rates." NBER Working Paper no. 15487, National Bureau of Economic Research, Cambridge, MA.

Watt, N. 2015. "Corbyn's Economic Strategy Would Keep Tories in Power, Top Labour Figure Says." *The Guardian*, August 3.

Weise, C. L. 2012. "Political Pressures on Monetary Policy during the US Great Inflation." *American Economic Journal: Macroeconomics* 4, no. 2 (April): 33–64.

Williamson, S. 2017. "Quantitative Easing: How Well Does This Tool Work?" Federal Reserve Bank of St. Louis *Regional Economist*, Third Quarter, August 18: 8–14.

Wren-Lewis, S. 2015a. "We Want Helicopters, and We Want Them . . . " *Mainly Macro* (blog), May 22.

———. 2015b. "People's QE and Corbyn's QE." *Mainly Macro* (blog), August 16.

Yates, T. 2015a. "Corbyn's QE for the People Jeopardises the Bank of England's Independence." *The Guardian*, September 22.

———. 2015b. "Helicopters and Slippery Slopes." *longandvariable* (blog), August 9.

ABOUT THE CATO INSTITUTE
AND ITS CENTER FOR MONETARY
AND FINANCIAL ALTERNATIVES

Founded in 1977, the Cato Institute is a public policy research foundation dedicated to broadening the parameters of policy debate to allow consideration of more options that are consistent with the principles of limited government, individual liberty, and peace.

The Institute is named for *Cato's Letters*, libertarian pamphlets that were widely read in the American Colonies in the early 18th century and played a major role in laying the philosophical foundation for the American Revolution.

The Cato Institute undertakes an extensive publications program on the complete spectrum of policy issues. Books, monographs, and shorter studies are commissioned to examine the federal budget, Social Security, regulation, military spending, international trade, and myriad other issues. Major policy conferences are held throughout the year.

The Cato Institute's Center for Monetary and Financial Alternatives was founded in 2014 to assess the shortcomings of existing monetary and financial regulatory arrangements, and to discover and promote more stable and efficient alternatives.

In order to maintain its independence, the Cato Institute accepts no government funding. Contributions are received from foundations, corporations, and individuals, and other revenue is generated from the sale of publications. The Institute is a nonprofit, tax-exempt, educational foundation under Section 501(c)3 of the Internal Revenue Code.

CATO INSTITUTE
1000 Massachusetts Avenue NW
Washington, DC 20001
www.cato.org

Printed in the USA
CPSIA information can be obtained
at www.ICGtesting.com
LVHW051632060124
768257LV00003B/215

9 781948 647939